A Hands-On
Manual for
Social Work
RESEARCH

Related books of interest

**Research Methods for Social Workers:
A Practice-Based Approach, Second Edition**
Samuel S. Faulkner and Cynthia A. Faulkner

**Doing Research: The Hows and Whys of Applied Research,
Third Edition**
Nel Verhoeven

A Practical Guide to Evaluation, Second Edition
Carl F. Brun

**Social Work Evaluation: Enhancing What We Do,
Second Edition**
James R. Dudley

The Community Needs Assessment Workbook
Rodney A. Wambeam

**Using Statistical Methods in Social Work Practice with a
Complete SPSS Guide, Second Edition**
Soleman H. Abu-Bader

A Hands-On Manual for Social Work

RESEARCH

Amy Catherine
Russell
Texas State University

LYCEUM
BOOKS, INC.
Chicago, IL 60637

© 2014 by Lyceum Books, Inc.

Published by

LYCEUM BOOKS, INC.
5758 S. Blackstone Avenue
Chicago, Illinois 60637
773-643-1903 fax
773-643-1902 phone
lyceum@lyceumbooks.com
www.lyceumbooks.com

6 5 4 3 2   14 15 16 17 18

ISBN 978-1-935871-72-9

Printed in the United States of America.

Library of Congress Cataloging-in-Publication Data

Russell, Amy Catherine.
    A hands-on manual for social work research / Amy Catherine Russell, Texas State University.
        pages cm
    Includes bibliographical references and index.
    ISBN 978-1-935871-72-9
    1. Social work education—Fieldwork. 2. Social service—Research—Methodology. 3. Social service—Fieldwork I. Title.
    HV11.R86 2015
    361.0072—dc23
                                    2014021890

Dedicated to my social work students who taught me that research confidence lies in access and application, not in impressive terms and design, and that the doing of research should be practical and fun.

Contents

List of Illustrations

List of Worksheets

1

Purpose of This Manual

YES, RESEARCH CAN BE SEXY! This is the tagline that this author has used over years of teaching research to students who sometimes dread the topic or find it irrelevant to social work because they mostly intend to become direct practitioners and find the gap between field work and research daunting. Interactions with students, undergraduate and graduate alike, have shown that, for research to be sexy, or usable and relevant to future career needs, it must be simple, accessible, and practical. That is the intention of this book, which can be used in its entirety as a research manual or for access to stand-alone topical areas with worksheets that will help students to attain their potential to conduct research in practice settings, particularly in program evaluation services.

> *Did you know that the less capable students feel when entering a research course, the greater the amount of confidence they can achieve in their research learning?*
> *(Unrau & Grinnell, 2005)*

This research manual originated from an idea (and from a few years of adapting to change) of how to best deliver and help students understand research in the context of program evaluation. The author has been teaching research, statistics, and evaluation for nearly eight years and has created a system of worksheets to this end, in a step-by-step format, to guide students through the process of evaluation research. In this process, she has found that the concept of less is more truly helps students to decrease their anxiety about the topic while they learn in an experiential manner. In addition to worksheets, the author has secured agency partnerships and other data sources to provide students a real-world research project. These resources will give students applications for evaluation learning, as well as opportunities for community service and service learning. This route is a means to develop students' capacity for using their skills in future social work careers, most likely in direct practice settings. Simply put, this workbook and text represent the author's attempt to deliver challenging content, in a subject that social work students are not so enthusiastic about, in an experiential and engaging way.

There are three main purposes of this research manual: (1) to present the evaluation (as research in the field) in the simplest format, (2) to present the undergirding research process in the simplest format, and (3) to present experiential learning opportunities and ideas to show students that they can conduct research. One of the more challenging but essential components of the course is mentoring students through the process as they conduct a living research project. To meet this challenge, the instructor will present content and exercises during the first half of the course and then meet with students individually and in groups during the second half. This will allow students privacy to ask specific project-related questions that they may feel uncomfortable raising among their peers; it will also allow them personal and directed time with the instructor, as well as opportunities to receive reassurance from the instructor. The instructor will use a Socratic method during this mentoring time, asking what students want to investigate and what they find interesting, and using a method of questions and answers to establish the best process for their evaluation research project.

> *In research done by the author, students state the enthusiasm of and rapport with the instructor increased their own enthusiasm as well as their research learning.*

All content for this research manual is written to the assignment, as contained in the "how to" worksheets. This narrative is addressed to both students and instructors. All content focuses on what is most common and realistic in social work program evaluation—what is "expected" in data available from nonprofit public welfare social services. As a disclaimer, this manual is written less in the context of pure evaluation and more in the context of applied research; the focus is on doing research, and as such it is the student who will make it real. This book is not a traditional evaluation text and does not focus on the technical formalities of the evaluation process, but instead uses the practice of data analysis and outcomes as the focus of student learning of research.

Because of this focus, the content is intended to be direct and practical, using mid-level research design and a utilitarian approach to outcome measurement. This focus includes a practice-based research perspective (Faulkner & Faulkner, 2014; Peake & Epstein, 2004) and an agency-directed, agency-need approach to evaluation so that outcomes are usable and determined by the agency to be appropriate for use in soliciting future funding.

This manual is directed at multiple levels of education, depending on the degree of interaction with the instructor. Although it is intended mainly for graduate-level and even doctoral students, where less instructor direction is beneficial, a more hands-on approach can be used for undergraduate students. How the manual is used, in its various formats, is completely up to the instructor. The main point is that teaching through the manual can involve either more interaction or less interaction depending on the level of education. No matter how the manual is applied by the instructor and the student, it should be remembered that the focus of the content is the relationship and interaction between student and instructor; it's a mutual relationship.

The author's ultimate goal is to provide a package of materials for students and instructors, including an evaluation research assignment, teaching methods, and student materials for experiential evaluation learning. Within this package are exercises for both student and instructor to deconstruct anxiety-provoking terms into their simplest form, and to provide just enough information and instruction for students to complete real-time research with skill and confidence. An essential part of this process is adaptability to student needs and learning formats, and from the author's own experience, one such format is repetition. The intent of this package is to provide the easiest access to research and evaluation because this access is essential to social justice, for both social work students and social welfare agencies. Finally, instructors using this book are encouraged to never apologize for teaching research and to never conceal how much they love it: this factor in itself can increase student learning. The instructor can be the perfect research role model.

2 A Different Perspective of Research and Evaluation

THE TERM *EVALUATION* AS USED in this manual specifically refers to field-related research, structural inquiry so to speak, that is conducted in practice settings, such as program evaluation for social services. The intent is not to present evaluation in its more formal and technical foundations, but to make it a research process accessible to students. Many nonprofits and social service entities do not have the resources, or manpower, for data management, data collection, outcome measurement, and reporting. This manual addresses how students can conduct research in such settings as a service to social and public welfare, providing support for interventions that will promote continued delivery and potential future funding. Any student, or executive director for that matter, knows that outcome research is essential to the continued life of a social service and to the support resources needed to deliver its programs and services. This research manual addresses such program evaluation tools and skills in a practice-based and field-related context. The author will attempt to deliver this content to match as closely as possible what students are doing in social work practice settings while integrating concepts and applications of program evaluation into a hands-on research study. The context of evaluation in this manual is social work practice research, in the simplest format possible for access by both social

5

service providers and students alike. The most important intent of this book is to make evaluation functional.

Although many program evaluation textbooks begin with chapters on accountability and cultural competence, this book will begin instead with brief surveys of historical changes in social service funding, the transition from public to private services, and the presumed hesitation to use standardized measurements. These first course sessions will conclude with perspectives on the marginalization of social service agencies and on the need for change from the current perception of social welfare agencies as social welfare clients (because they lack positive recognition and adequate funding) to a more empowerment and strengths-based perception that includes participatory action research (Greenwood & Levin, 2007). These class sessions are intended to introduce students to the political processes of evaluation and the ideology behind money and grants, as well as to provide a historical overview of the current situation, thus exposing them to different perspectives on evaluation, and hopefully encouraging sensitivity to the persons administering and receiving social services.

HISTORICAL FOUNDATIONS OF ACCOUNTABILITY

Since the Reagan Administration passed financial policy to support *trickle-down economics* (to the dismay of economists who warned against this policy; see Karger and Stoesz, 2009), spending for social welfare has been made part of a block allocation (i.e., block grants) and transferred from federal government to state governments for dispersal as they see fit to fund public welfare agencies. Although trickle-down economics has been shown to be flawed in the concept that, if the rich are sufficiently well-off, they will give to the poor, the attitude, as well as the funding policy, remains: spending on public welfare should be boxed in a package and given to the states. This process has decreased the funding for public welfare and social service programs. It has also invited in a currently well-known mechanism known as charitable giving and fundraising for such giving, on which many social service agencies now rely. Furthermore, it has created, over the ensuing years, an incredible increase in oversight over agencies receiving federal monies dispersed from state legislation. Social services were, and are, answering to many masters while funding has decreased. Funding that was once stable and reliable and came from the federal government changed into decreased funding from the state with many regulations and accountability measures attached, as if delivering the service to the public did not represent sufficient accountability.

> *Should decreasing a social service's rolls be considered an effective or accountable program mechanism? Read more about the Personal Responsibility and Work Opportunity Reconciliation Act in Karger & Stoesz (2009).*

Although the author is not arguing against accountability in social services, she is trying to present a different perspective. Institutions that receive public monies to provide public services should show that this money is being spent as intended and that an effective service is being provided. However, does accountability to many masters divert needed resources from service delivery to administrative bean counting and an overanalysis of a simple service and intervention delivery? Is accountability one way to divert resources from persons in need?

Perhaps accountability can be viewed in a fresh way, such as providing service evaluation in an empowered manner, not in a conditional or even summative way, but in a way that promotes and markets outcomes. If instead of swooping in and making external generalizations about how an agency should be run, the evaluator commended the agency for providing a service with such little money, just think of the potential in empowered outcomes. With the empowerment model, the evaluator does not assume expertise in the delivery of services, or in evaluation and research, but works with the agency to help it delineate and analyze these outcomes.

History explains what agencies are working with, and without, and gives an interesting spin on the concept of accountability. Seeing a bigger picture and understanding that all things come from policy, even evaluation and accountability, is essential in knowing how to conduct this very important research for public welfare agencies.

Sensitivity may be required when discussing accountability as it pertains to social agencies. Caution is required when jumping on the accountability bandwagon, particularly in terms of blaming and commenting about why a social service doesn't do this or that and especially when the agency is operating with little and providing much. Accountability in terms of how public welfare recipients and the agencies that provide social services are treated may be better perceived. In some places there is a conditioned attitude of blaming and distrust of public agencies, especially those that serve persons who cannot "pull themselves up by their bootstraps." All would be better served in an empowerment model of evaluation. This could provide a practical application for the research process as well as a means of improving services, service delivery, and agency-based, client-directed interventions.

Historical foundations of accountability are more accurately explanations of why we do not have enough money to run these agencies. Perhaps the issue of accountability is best addressed by social work schools that train evaluation researchers to ensure that evaluation outcomes are generated in a productive manner. Keep in mind that this is just a small perspective on history; the issue is truly complex and many other factors have come into play in the discussion of social service accountability. Power and perspective are definitive points to consider in this discussion.

> *Did you know that fewer master's students are returning to earn their PhDs, compared proportionately to those graduating (Council on Social Work Education, 2011)? Think of the increased need for PhD-level social workers and social work evaluators in the near future.*

PUBLIC TO PRIVATE

As another history lesson in accountability, social services in the past were delivered by public agencies, without an agenda of profit. Public services were truly public, delivered by the state and usually supported by the federal government and provided to persons with low or no income (Fisher & Karger, 1996). There have been multiple attempts, some successful, to privatize public services. For example, Medicare D undid well-established federal government mechanisms to negotiate lower priced pharmaceuticals for seniors and public welfare recipients (Karger & Stoesz, 2009). Companies assumed this responsibility in a for-profit endeavor, creating new conditions, rules, and regulations for service recipients.

Working with social services in an evaluation capacity, social work students and instructors will see nonprofits competing with for-profits to provide the same service, although in the end it may not be the original service. Increasingly, social services are having to restrict services to those with certain insurances, and due to funding cuts, are decreasing their capacity to provide service to those with no public help, insurance, or services. This has allowed private for-profits to bid on service delivery. There is also an increase in contracted work and services partitioned out from public agencies as cost-saving measures. Services formerly available to all now may require the fulfillment of a set of conditions, or characteristics, and may be delivered by an entity making a profit from the consumer's not-so-public encounter. Business models of competition, contracting services for cost savings, and corporate mentalities of mainstreaming and quantification have not been a traditional strength of social and public services, although this is exactly what is happening in present-day service delivery. In view of the change from public to private services, evaluators must be sensitive to the strains and stresses experienced by nonprofits.

As an example of the public to private issue in these first sessions, students should be asked to observe their universities. Are their universities accountable to them, are services that were once public now private, and did students provide input on these changes? If there was no participation from students in these changes, then there is a gap in accountability.

CULTURAL COMPETENCE IN EVALUATION

Throughout modern history, in any measurement endeavor, even in the first stage development theories of such a diverse group as gay, lesbian, bisexual, and transgender (GLBT) persons, standardized instrumentation and measurement, those instruments considered reliable and valid, have traditionally been normed on white males. The list of instruments ranges from the SAT and GRE to depression and anger inventories. Although efforts have been made to increase diverse learning and cultural understandings, they do not change the initial intention or purpose of such testing instruments. Standardized tests may be the safeguard in social service delivery and graduate school admissions, but they may not be fair to all those who take them.

With this knowledge, students soliciting and conducting evaluation research in a social service will want to consider how best to keep cultural sensitivity primary. One way to do this is to ask the agency to provide the instruments that it presently uses for measurement. Even if the agency has no measurement for pretesting and posttesting, it may have a database. Ultimately it is best and most culturally competent to allow the agency to determine the best measurement for service recipients. If social work students are bilingual and have knowledge of racism and some graphic design skills, they can provide input to an improved and accessible measurement for the population served; this direction needs to come from the service providers and service recipients themselves. Another route to increased cultural competence is helping the agency and participants design such measurements themselves; following the ideas of those who are affected should be essential in creating the program, policy, or intervention (Chapin, 1995, 2011; Gibbons & Gray, 2005). This would be ideal. An additional component of cultural sensitivity is insider research (LaSala, 2003), for example, evaluations of internships or work settings by student interns. The student has inside knowledge of the workings of his or her organization, and as an insider, can easily ask for feedback from service recipients in designing outcome measures. When working with agencies, in whatever context, student researchers should consider the ethical issues and refer to the social work code of conduct when they question the ethical implications that arise. If such questions arise, the instructor and agency contact/executive director are the most immediate resources.

THE SILVER LINING

Considering scarcity of resources, vulnerability to policy changes, service reductions, and historical marginalization of clients and agencies can make a student, instructor, or executive director of a nonprofit feel overwhelmed and unmotivated, uninspired, and ready to give up. However, knowledge of history and policy is salient in evaluation research; students need some general conceptualization of how history has played a part in current times and an understanding of what problems social workers have faced. In these first sessions of gloom and doom, students must be challenged to change their perspective. Perceiving a social service agency as a client and knowing how society and even governmental ideologies marginalize social services in the same way that they marginalize clients may provide a perspective of empowerment and strengths-based social work, even in evaluation services. Knowing the challenges faced by nonprofit agencies in delivering their services can allow students, instructors, and other stakeholders to be more sensitive to the needs of these agencies as well as to provide evaluation in a more empowering way.

Without an understanding of history and the explanation of why things are as they are, evaluators and students may not truly understand the best sensitivities to bring to a social service when evaluating its outcomes. History also provides knowledge of how money has become scarce and how nonprofits compete for scarce resources.

> *Did you know that the need for social workers is expected to increase by 25 percent over the next decade (Bureau of Labor Statistics, 2012)? Just think how the negotiating power of social workers entering the field will change, including salary negotiations.*

Viewing research within agencies as an outcome, as opposed to an evaluation, may help external, or even internal, evaluators to decrease some apprehension in the investigative and inquiry process. If evaluators, or outcomes researchers, allowed for agency-directed and agency-driven participatory action research, evaluation itself could become a more coordinated, advocacy-directed, and promoting endeavor. Just a simple shift into a different perspective of evaluation could result in a new foundation of outcome measurement, a more positive and empowering process. Above all, the research work provided to agencies needs to be useful to them and to the clients they serve. For example, knowing that most nonprofit public social services are competing for grant monies, what if evaluation services helped agencies to believe that they could attain, and hence work toward, the resources needed? What if the evaluation researcher helped agencies believe that there is enough money for all social services to be adequately funded, and that there is a pot of gold to support the livelihood of helping others? Radical.

3 Methods

THE ZEN OF RESEARCH DESIGN: BEING OK WITH HOW THIS THING FALLS OUT

THE INTENTION OF THE COURSE and evaluation research project is to have students complete a true research study within a semester. With this in mind, the first few weeks will require some instructor presence to make arrangements for data; this process can be anxiety provoking because instructor and student are unsure of just what is contained within the potential data from a social service agency. The author finds the first month of class to be the *reassurance stage* in which she encourages students to be patient and assures them that the evaluation will fall out perfectly if they trust in the process, even though at this point they have no idea of what data they will be analyzing nor how to even begin a literature review.

The first assignment and focus is the Methods section, seen as a proposal rather than a sure thing. If students propose what they will do in the program evaluation, there is more freedom to adjust to the needs of the social service. Similarly, this approach decreases some anxiety that results from the lack of knowing exactly what the student will be evaluating. Think of methods as a proposal design, which is really what everyone does when drawing up methods: they have not started the study yet, and they are simply explaining their intentions of research. Such a process can be navigated in worksheet 3.1 below.

> *In an impromptu study of this instructor's advanced MSW research course, students stated they expected to know more ahead of time about research terminology and skills than they would in a direct practice course.*

Worksheet 3.1

RESEARCH PROCESS:
Planning to Answer Your Research Question

I. Preliminary Issues:
Is there an area/subject/concept that really interests you? It could be in your work, a group that really intrigues you, a recurring question that pops into your head, a cause you want to advocate for—anything. It could be something you are passionate about, something you know about already, something you want to know more about, or even something that is totally unknown.

Think about how to narrow this interest into a smaller realm. What is it about? Who is involved? What is the problem you see or don't see?

Think about the questions that arise when you observe something, hear something, or simply have those wandering musings. Do you already have a hypothetical/preliminary prediction or guess about the nature of this problem? What is this guess based on?

Most importantly, your research question should interest you and/or have a bearing on your life, career, or education, for example. You will invest a lot of time pondering this question; let it be something you are willing to invest time in.

Name a general problem area or issue that interests you. At this point, your problem area/issue may still be broad or it may be narrow. Note that you may want to name several problem areas for research and make a final decision later.

Have you already made personal observations related to this problem/issue? If so, briefly describe your observations. Did you make informal observations? Did you plan this in a more structured way and decide in advance who to observe and how and when to observe?

II. What Type of Method Would Best Investigate Your Question?

If you wanted to conduct a future study on your problem/issue of interest, would you use an inductive or deductive process? Could it be both?

In thinking about how you might conduct a future study on your problem/issue, what sort of research design might you use? If it is experimental, what treatments and/or manipulated variables might you use?

Will a control group be necessary? If not, why not? Should the study be a pilot study? Why?

If it is nonexperimental, will it be ex post facto or retrospective (looking to the past for causes of a current condition)? Why is a nonexperimental design more appropriate to study your problem/issue than an experimental design?

What type of nonexperimental study will it be (survey, case study, ethnography, longitudinal, or other nonexperimental design)?

For the research question that you are asking, what are the major variables? The dependent variable? The independent variable(s)? What variables are quantitative?

III. How Will You Ask Your Question(s)?
State the purpose of a potential study that you might conduct on your topic, a general research question that guides the study, and/or a possible research hypothesis (you may have more than one).

How will you define, operationalize, and measure the variables involved in your research question?

Will you be evaluating a program in your research? If yes, name the program and indicate whether the evaluation will be formative or summative.

Do you anticipate that research on your topic has the potential to harm the participants? How would it cause harm (loss of privacy, etc.)? What measures can be used to guard against possible harm?

Is informed consent necessary? Who should review your consent form? Who should grant approval to conduct the study?

Is this study intended to help or advocate for a certain population? How?

Is your research question interesting, creative, or controversial? How?

IV. What Have Other People Said About This Type of Question?

Is the purpose of your study to test a hypothesis deduced from theory? Or is the purpose of your study to make observations on which a theory may be built?

Have you begun reading the literature in your problem area? If yes, are there previous studies on this topic? If yes, are you planning a strict replication of a previous study, a modified replication, or a study that might resolve conflict with the literature? How?

Was your research question or hypothesis based on the literature that you have read?

List some key words you might use in an electronic search of the literature.

Have you started writing a literature review on the topic? Have the findings from previous studies addressed your question? Have the findings from these previous studies been contradictory? Have these previous studies utilized appropriate methods? If so, what might account for the differences in the findings?

Have you picked certain concepts from certain theories to integrate into your review? If yes, why did you choose these particular concepts? Are you excluding any concepts that others have looked at? Why?

Have you started making a reference list based on American Psychological Association (APA) format?

What are the strengths and weaknesses of your proposed study? What are the contributions it will make to the field? What are the implications for practice, policy, basic research, etc.?

Secondary data acquisition is a feasible option within a semester because it will expedite institutional review board (IRB) exemption and eliminate the time needed for more detailed knowledge of design method, participant recruitment, and data collection. The IRB is the ethics committee for most universities. However, this is only one option for content delivery; additional options will be discussed in chapter 5. For the single-semester option, students have four choices for possible studies: (1) secondary data from a previous student internship, another faculty member, or a community contact; (2) secondary data acquired by the instructor from local social service agencies; (3) secondary data from larger (perhaps federal) databases (such as the NLSY79); and (4) secondary data that the instructor has collected but not yet analyzed. Again, it is salient that data are secondary, archival, and historical to ensure the completion of a research study within a semester.

Did you know you are constantly collecting and analyzing data? Consider this example. Before registering for this course, you may have asked around about the professor to determine if you wanted to take said professor. Sitting in said professor's class, you are collecting data about the assignment, observing the professor's interactions, and analyzing your opportunities to earn an A. Information collected on course and professor are data; the analysis will tell you, based on the data, if you are likely to earn an A.

Based on the author's experience, unless contacts are made in advance, liaison and coordination of data sources will consume the first month of a semester and will require meeting with executive directors of local social services, including planning for students to meet later with agency contacts to enter and then analyze the secondary data. This is when the Zen comes in: the process of data acquisition and explanation to both agency contacts and students requires much reassurance and patience. Students must understand that it is the process of interacting and helping agencies that is important, not the immediacy of acquisition or foresight into the outcomes. Explain to students that being OK with how this thing falls out is very important, not just at the beginning of the semester, but throughout the semester. Reassure them also that they will not be graded on the size of their sample, the significance of their statistical tests, or the earth-shattering nature of their outcomes. It's the journey, not the destination, or it's the process, not the outcome (sample size, statistical significance, and earth-shattering outcomes). Trust the process of research learning in an experiential way, and enjoy providing a free service to agencies that more than likely do not have evaluation resources.

Terms

At this juncture, students often find that they don't remember, or don't want to remember, that research course they took in preparation for their bachelor's degree in social work (BSW), or perhaps that they don't have a sufficient command from their foundation research course for their master's in social work (MSW). This is when the instructor will spend a few class sessions refreshing students on terminology and methodology, including some in-class exercises.

It is essential to deconstruct research methods and terms and increase the ease with which they can be understood. Consider the enigma and mystery surrounding those fancy research terms, and your fear that you'll never grasp such high-level and sophisticated non-social-work-related scientific phraseology, such as ANOVA, explanatory, reliability, and validity. Those terms sound so technical, intimidating, and otherworldly. No, they are not, really! All you need to know about such terms is the easiest way to remember them, mainly for your purposes in program evaluation. The way to simplify them and ease the learning process is to deconstruct and break apart every research term, using some simple English concepts and related words to tell you exactly what they mean. Consider these as examples:

- Quantitative: *quantity*, or how much, numbers, counts, frequencies, numerical data.

- Qualitative: *quality*, or words, deeper meanings, text, and narrative data.

- Correlation: how two things *relate* to each other.

- ANOVA: *ANalysis Of VAriance*, a stats test that analyzes group differences.

- Explanatory: *to explain* a thing through the most rigorous research method.

- Reliability: *reliable;* can you trust it, as in a precise, well-used measurement?

- Validity: *valid;* can you trust that measurement to exactly measure your concept in a larger research study?

- Probability: is it *probable*? Selection by equal chance for everyone.

- Operationalization: to make something *operational,* such as an instrument that breaks down conceptual ideas into items that can be measured in numbers or words.

Not so scary now, perhaps? The point is, yes, it is this easy; these terms are exactly what they say they are, and the foundation of their meaning is unchanging. With such knowledge and confidence, you can then add more to the terms. For example, validity means is a thing valid; can you trust it? Is the measurement assessing your concept in a larger research study? Is the study valid? Have you chosen the correct measurement to assess the concepts within your research study?

Design Symbols

The process of refreshing and re-familiarizing students with research and terminology begins with terms and then progresses to methodology and design. Other intimidating items in research tend to be the symbols used for design, e.g., R for randomization and O_1 for pretest. The instructor will write these symbols on the board as he or she explains them, going back and forth to provide further explanation as students ask questions. It is a bit of a brain-washing process, but keeping it simple is helpful. For example, the primary symbols for all research design boil down to just these:

- R = random assignment to a control (C) group and a treatment (TX) group

- O_1 = the dependent variable (DV), the first observation of it, a pretest

- X = the intervention, the independent variable (IV)

- O_2 = the dependent variable (DV) again, the second observation of it, a posttest

Put these symbols together and what you have is a traditional program evaluation design:

- X O_1 the one-shot, one-group, cross-sectional study, or

- O_1 X O_2 the one-group pretest and posttest, cross-sectional study

Then if you're lucky, you might even have this:

TX O_1 X_1 O_2
C O_1 X_2 O_2

Note that the C implies comparison, not control group; X_1 is the intervention you are investigating; and X_2 is another or similar comparative intervention received by a different group of participants. This all depends on the data a social service has collected; many do not have the resources to conduct both pretest and posttest, or even the instrumentation to measure changes in a posttest, but they may have counts (frequencies) of services received and types of services, for example, and these counts may be in qualitative form (words = progress notes).

It is helpful to add that student researchers will not likely be using the R (random assignment) unless they have miraculous sample size resources, are conducting their own research with millions in federal grant dollars, or perhaps have a larger secondary data set and can randomly select, which in effect is not really good enough for a true experimental method. What will probably happen is that there will be one group receiving an intervention or the treatment that we want to know about.

As an example, your instructor has dry hair that is neither bouncy nor lively (the DV, O_1, the first observation of the dependent variable). She decides to do something about this because she really wants bouncy hair so she runs out and buys the commercialized Super Duper Bouncy Shampoo (IV, X, the intervention is shampoo). She washes, rinses, and repeats as instructed for four days. On the fourth day, she observes her hair to see if it has the bouncy liveliness that was promised by the product marketing (the DV, O_2, the second observation of the dependent variable). Nope, the professor still has dry hair that is neither bouncy nor lively, even after applying the intervention of the shampoo. It would then be safe to say that, for this participant, the intervention was not effective. Bummer. Perhaps she can at least get her money back, or try another shampoo.

So the question is, and it is usually a research question, not a hypothesis for which we know more and have a more rigorous, experimental method: Is the intervention working? This is the program evaluation research purpose. This is the main focus for the entire study, in one sentence, using a few terms and a few symbols.

Design Methods

Putting the terms and symbols together allows you to move on to the next stage, which is design methodology: the symbols and organization that describe how the DV and IV are measured will help you define the exact method to be used. The three research method designs are diagrammed below, in a more deconstructed and applicable form, in which evaluation for practical purposes will mainly fall into categories of exploratory and pre-experimental or quasi-experimental (or descriptive or correlational) design methodology. Experimental/explanatory research design requires many conditions to be met, including randomized groups, random sampling, and lots of interval/ratio levels of measurements, to name a few. It is more than likely that the evaluator does not have the opportunity or time to use such a rigorous method. This does not mean that exploratory and pre-experimental methods do not have conditions; they do have conditions, but they work better with a social work evaluation mentality and have more wiggle room to adjust as needed to the available, or unavailable, data.

The research method is simply the description of how you will go about the program evaluation study, and it is usually an educated guess ahead of time because you may not have access to the data, or know exactly what data the social service has. It is more than likely that the methods used by the social service to conduct and deliver the intervention. and even the way it is measured, are unknown. Design means taking your symbols ($O_1 X O_2$) and linearly drawing out their progression in time, to the best of your ability ahead of time. It is simply the picture of your study in symbols and terms. For a traditional and expected program, the evaluation method is usually the one-group, cross-sectional, pretest and posttest design. This design resides in the realm of the exploratory and pre-experimental, or descriptive, research methods, shown in figure 3.1.

IT'S ALL ABOUT THE DATA

Evaluation is about looking at data, and data are simply bits of information. Data are measures of a participant's behavior within

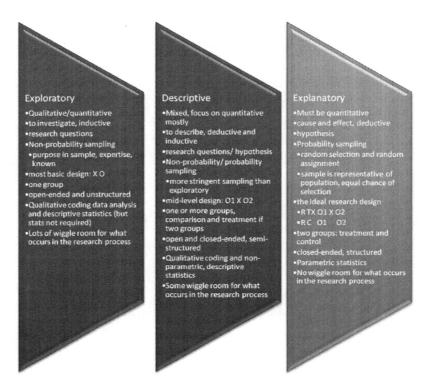

Exploratory
- Qualitative/quantitative
- to investigate, inductive
- research questions
- Non-probability sampling
  - purpose in sample, expertise, known
- most basic design: X O
- one group
- open-ended and unstructured
- Qualitative coding data analysis and descriptive statistics (but stats not required)
- Lots of wiggle room for what occurs in the research process

Descriptive
- Mixed, focus on quantitative mostly
- to describe, deductive and inductive
- research questions/ hypothesis
- Non-probability/ probability sampling
  - more stringent sampling than exploratory
- mid-level design: O1 X O2
- one or more groups, comparison and treatment if two groups
- open and closed-ended, semi-structured
- Qualitative coding and non-parametric, descriptive statistics
- Some wiggle room for what occurs in the research process

Explanatory
- Must be quantitative
- cause and effect, deductive
- hypothesis
- Probability sampling
  - random selection and random assignment
  - sample is representative of population, equal chance of selection
- the ideal research design
  - R TX O1 X O2
  - R C O1   O2
- two groups: treatment and control
- closed-ended, structured
- Parametric statistics
- No wiggle room for what occurs in the research process

FIGURE 3.1 DESIGN DIAGRAM: The Three Design Methods

an intervention: how the participant reacts, responds, or feels about it. Data can answer the research question for all program evaluations: does the intervention help the clients? Data can take many forms, preferably a measurement that acts as a receptacle for information, such as how a person feels upon entering an intervention (DV, O_1, pretest) and how he or she feels after the intervention (DV, O_2, posttest). This measurement, instrument, and/or survey asks questions of a participant, who decides on the basis of his or her attitudes, knowledge, and feelings what fits his or her experience of the intervention. For example, a student collects information about a research course and assesses her feelings about whether she will survive it. She then needs to design a method for measuring her feelings about research course survival. One way to do so is with a Likert scale (social workers love Likert scales), which is simply an ordinal scale that ranks responses; it is not a type of survey, but an instrument used by researchers to measure responses, or to add levels or degrees to responses. Table 3.1 is a Likert scale with Likert-type response items.

TABLE 3.1 LIKERT RESPONSES

	Response			
I am going to survive advanced research	*Strongly agree*	*Agree*	*Disagree*	*Strongly disagree*

A pretest (and posttest, which must be the same as the pretest to allow comparison) may be a series of questions regarding a similar group of things, such as a series of questions related to how one survives an advanced research course. Pretests and posttests can show in a very simple way how a person feels, thinks, or comprehends an intervention. In this case, the intervention, or independent variable, is the taking of an advanced research course. The dependent variable, the before (pretest) and after (posttest) observation of how the student feels or thinks about advanced research, is simply the measurement, or a way to collect data and information about such thoughts and feelings. The data are collected on an ordinal level of measurement; they are ordered, ranked, and rated, but response items such as *strongly agree* cannot be measured with a number. We do know that *strongly agree* is more than *agree*, but the difference cannot be measured with a number. We are talking about *levels of measurement* now, which describe how data, such as a student's feelings about surviving an advanced research course, are collected and measured. Levels of measurement are for quantitative data only. There are four levels of measurement, but in statistics the difference between interval (a real number) and ratio (a real number that includes absolute zero) is unimportant; they are used interchangeably in the Statistical Package for the Social Sciences (SPSS), and the interval/ratio level of measurement is called scale in SPSS. Levels of measurement are listed in table 3.2 with easy ways to remember them.

TABLE 3.2 LEVELS OF MEASUREMENT

Level of measurement	Type of measurement	Example	Coding
Nominal	Name	Male or female: yes or no	Code for stats (1 = yes, 0 = no)
Ordinal	Order	Strongly agree or strongly disagree: freshman, sophomore, junior, senior	Code (4 = *strongly agree* . . . 1 = *strongly disagree*)
Interval/ratio	Continuous intervals and ratios	Age, weight, IQ, inches and feet, fractions	Real numbers (25 years old = 25 years old)

Now that we have data—quantitative data, in this case—or simply information, we take these data and measure them by assigning meaning through levels of measurement, which are the codes and numbers assigned to response items, such as ranks or real numbers. There are two types of data that work well for program evaluation. One is new data that you collect yourself as a researcher, for example, by using a pretest and posttest to measure how well an intervention works. The other type of data have already been collected by an agency using some sort of measurement, such as a pretest and/or posttest, intake, progress note, or even counts of services rendered; these are called secondary data (similar to archival and historical data). Secondary data can be analyzed and written up in a report during a semester, and can be much easier and faster to use than newly collected data.

Sampling

Sampling in secondary data analysis is normally non-probability and purposive. Because the data have been collected previously, the evaluator has no control over the sampling techniques. Programs and agencies tend to assess all those who participate in an intervention; hence, unlike probability sampling, there is no systematic sampling used. Because all persons receiving an intervention are requested to participate, there is intention and no chance associated with this sampling, and therefore it is non-probability sampling. Additionally, because the goal is to survey and assess outcomes from a group receiving a specific intervention, this is purposive sampling as well. The particular group receiving the intervention has been purposefully surveyed.

Probability sampling fits with experimental research, which social work conducts in a minimalistic manner to avoid denying treatment by utilizing control groups, or placing participants on waiting lists for a treatment because of the ethical concerns associated with doing so. Social workers tend to assess and measure what is occurring and to use exploratory and mid-level research designs that are more fitting to interventions and applied research. Random selection probability sampling requires two groups to be selected from a random sample; participants are then placed by chance into one of two groups, also called randomization. Although it is non-normative in social work research, random selection can be accomplished in secondary data by using a random numbers chart to select cases from a larger sample, for example. However, use of non-probability and purposive sampling is safer and easier to explain in program evaluation research because it fits better with the purposes of practice-based social work research.

Soliciting Agencies for Data: Hitting the Jackpot

Somewhere out there, just waiting for you to find it, residing within a local social service agency, is a closet full of boxes and boxes of data—the jackpot. Although exciting to the instructor or evaluator, this jackpot may be overwhelming to the student. Once this closet of boxes is secured for data entry and analysis, the instructor will start assigning those boxes to students for database creation and data entry. This is what Epstein (2001) calls *data mining,* and is the perfect example of practice-based research. Although students may be sent out to enter and analyze existing, already secured data (i.e., secondary data), the liaison within the agency will direct the student evaluator to said data. Because the agency liaison has knowledge of existing research and practice documentation, and knows what needs analysis within this documentation, this then is an exercise in practice-based research.

Because the agency liaison has ties to collected secondary data, he or she will know what needs analysis, entry, and interpretation for future funding and to show efficacious outcomes. The agency's practice is directing students' research. This also exposes students to the same concepts of practice-based research that they will apply to their future social work careers; they will become intimate with the data collected within their agency, and they will notice trends and patterns in changes or phenomena that they observe, hear, or think about while interacting with clients. From this knowledge of and direct experience with an intervention and/or agency, research and evaluation thoughts will arise. These ideas are much more useful for evaluation because they come from within, or inside, a social service delivery. This insider experience will lead to data and information collected by an agency that can answer research questions; locating these data is called data mining.

> *Although control groups and experimental designs increase the rigor of a study, they are not so feasible in evaluation and social work research. As an alternative, comparison groups, each receiving a similar intervention, may be used.*

Data mining (Epstein, 2001), the retrieval of data that can be used within an agency for evaluation outcomes, can include anything in practice-based research that the practitioner finds useful; such data may lie outside the closet of boxes in the form of progress notes, thank you notes, intakes, treatment plans, pretests and posttests, eligibility screening forms, counts of group participants, counts of services received, or even an already existing database—you name it, all records are data. Even previously analyzed data that are entered into a database for trends across time may be useful. Although already analyzed data may pose a more challenging research study, they are still valuable and are directed by the agency contact as desired for outcome measurement, again, a practice-based research tactic that is very helpful to the agency.

The basic social work skills apply to requests for data: allow agency liaisons to voice and share their opinions; remember empowerment and strengths-based perspectives, and let them tell you, because they know best, what they need and what outcomes are most meaningful and necessary for them. An explanation of the service to be provided and the preference for raw and unanalyzed data, such as pretests and posttests, is also important. Creation of a data management system, database, data entry, and data analysis is exactly what many agencies need for future funding and may not be able to do themselves due to resource and time constraints. It is important to think of this offer for outcome measurement as a gift, a service, and helpful to an agency. It is also helpful to provide the agency with a promotional tool after the analysis for marketing the intervention and promoting outcomes.

There is also another scenario, in which the agency has limited or no instrumentation for outcome assessment. Although all agencies, regardless of size, will have documentation of some sort, they may not have data collection tools in place for satisfaction, feedback, or follow-up surveys after services are delivered. Again, data mining helps because the agency knows what documentation it has, and from this knowledge, adaptations can be made and new measurements aligned with current documentation to create a satisfaction survey, some sort of evaluation measurement, and follow-up after clients exit services. Creativity comes into play here, and students can produce attitude surveys and learning and skill transference measurements, and ultimately truly learn applied research through the creation and administration of outcome measurement. This is discussed in more detail in chapter 5, "Data Management." Students can discover that their original research and more intimately designed research study can provide outcomes that are tailored to agency needs. That closet full of boxes is not a requirement of exceptional practice evaluation research.

INSTITUTIONAL REVIEW BOARD EXEMPTION: GETTING FAMOUS FROM YOUR RESEARCH STUDY

Once the data are acquired and both students and instructor have a better idea of the methods most relevant to the data, it is time to consider IRB exemption versus IRB approval. The author finds that secondary data analysis is not only easier to complete within a semester, as well as more helpful to agencies that have collected the data, but it also fits better with IRB exemption. If data collection methods require IRB approval, this can slow down the progression of the study and prevent students from completing it in one semester because of the time needed to develop a more rigorous and less flexible research protocol. Even without revisions, IRB approval takes time. A confidentiality form is included in appendix C for use in such a study by the student, instructor, and agency. This is not the only option, however; data collection and IRB or ethics committee approval can be sought for a two-semester or longer research study. Data collection can also be exempt from ethics/IRB review if there is no intention to publish the results.

> *Control groups are tricky in social work program evaluation. As social workers, we do not want to ever deny treatment for the sake of evidenced-based practice. Also, we do not usually have the opportunity to randomly select and assign groups. We are mostly retrospective evaluators, going in after treatment delivery to research the intervention.*

There are five federal categories of exemption, and secondary data analysis falls under category 4. Additionally, exemption from the full IRB approval process can be requested for program evaluation (category 5) and curriculum studies (category 1). What exemption provides is proof that the research study is on the up-and-up, and you still can publish, present, and promote the findings. However, it is essential to ensure that the exemption category (e.g., secondary data) does not change during the semester, which is a possibility in a more adaptive and agency-directed program evaluation. For example, students conducting research using any method, secondary or newly collected data, within a classroom setting, can do so without IRB approval or exemption, as long as the research is not published or presented. If exemption is given for secondary research, and students find that they are collecting data and doing scale development as requested by an agency, it is imperative that they do not publish or present, but give the findings and products back to the agency for its use. It is important to keep the IRB exemption as exact as possible, and in the more flexible agency-directed and practice-based research, to ensure that results are used in curriculum studies and for the agency only. An instructor can also use his or her own previous exemptions or approvals for students to conduct research during the semester-long project when working with the instructor's data.

Again, as mentioned above, IRB approval may be required for newly collected data or original research formulated by students, which is commonplace when designing and collecting first-time measurements. If the agency needs revolve around such survey creation and the administration and collection of new data, IRB approval is the safest route for future dissemination of results, as well as for publication. In this case, the project is best delivered over the course of two semesters because IRB approval usually mandates revisions to design and assurance that clients are protected. In the author's experience, the only way around applying for full IRB approval is to not publish the results, which is a decision that the student must make. An exemption can be sought and approved by the IRB for original research if the instructor and student state that they will not publish results in peer-reviewed journals. An expedited review can be requested if the design is simple and straightforward. A suggestion for collecting new data and conducting a more in-depth evaluation study is to simply extend the content delivery over two semesters to allow time for approval and data collection. This is discussed more in chapter 5.

WRITING FOR RESEARCH: OFF THE SOAPBOX

In an experiential learning environment, another initial consideration in the evaluation process is the transition from writing direct practice papers, which are more reflective and analytical, to writing research papers. Although the research paper is a requirement across the graduate curriculum, students may find it challenging to write in a more organized, exact, and technical manner. It is very important to present the research paper in a clean, concise way, using APA (American Psychological Association) style. Ensure that the paper is written in the third person, using technical and research terminology, in a neutral or impartial format, and is uniform and organized throughout. Students find it challenging at times to step off the soapbox of social injustice and down to earth in a "just the facts" format. To help in this transition, the instructor should spend class time explaining these requirements and the following items to students to orient them to research writing.

Formatting the paper correctly, using APA style (see Research Resources, appendix A) is the first step for students learning to write in a research tone. The author encourages students, when writing research papers, to use the following guidelines:

- Keep a sample APA manuscript nearby.

- Have a research book available to review terms that you may have forgotten or misunderstood.

- Avoid writing in very long sentences to make it easier to review your writing for clarity. Keep sentences short and simple.

- Use subheadings to assist the reader in navigating the content.

- Use statistics instead of verbal appeals to express the need for an intervention or program. Using neutral language rather than inducing guilt in the reader is a large and recurring issue. Winning over readers with numbers is more effective in a research paper than accusing them of not doing enough to rid the world of some evil. Leading the reader to your cause through eloquent expression and neutral language is more effective than making accusatory and blaming assertions. We want friends, not enemies, in our research endeavors.

■ And, most importantly, if you are not sure what you are saying, don't say it.

In this section, think of the methodology as a proposal. At this point, in the very early stages of the evaluation research study, you can determine the most likely way to go about the process and begin writing the methods. Following are a few more items to consider in the Methods section of a study:

1. Remember that evaluation research is a process; be patient and think of the methods as a proposal.
2. Don't be concerned with outcomes yet; we just began this thing!
3. Do wonder about what you want to know and wrap your query in a research question.
4. You are providing a free service to an agency; empower the agency as you would a client.
5. Be flexible about agency-directed needs and make changes as requested by the agency.
6. Using secondary data is the way to go.
7. Use research terms and deconstruct them to increase their access and usefulness.
8. Use design symbols: what are the IVs (interventions) and DVs (observations)?
9. Design the research method by combining items 6, 7, and 8 in an evaluation process: 6 + 7 + 8 = methods.
10. Focus on potential data sources and their possible levels of measurement.

11. Acquire secondary data from an agency; data mine for what the agency needs analyzed.
12. Write in neutral, "research-y," numerical formats; use APA style to keep your paper organized and pretty.

Worksheet 3.2 will help you walk through the methods process in a defined step-by-step way. But before you begin filling in the blanks, think about this: What if research was really easy?

Worksheet 3.2

HOW TO DO THE METHODS SECTION

Methods (use this as the heading for this section; subheadings are underlined and listed below). Blank lines are for you to fill in for the paper.

The purpose of the methods section is to tell your reader how you are doing the program evaluation, how you are answering the research question, and that as an external evaluator, you will be doing the research in a certain way (using a specific research design). The best design for evaluation research is the pretest and the posttest! You should also include the data collection methods (instruments), the participants (sample), and the lens (quantitative and/or qualitative) through which you will be examining the data. Be sure to use those research terms and techniques! This is a formal section; it is technical and you want to give enough information to future researchers so that they can replicate what you have done. A step-by-step explanation is given below:

1. Introduction to your methods section: Make a smooth transition from the end of the literature review (see

worksheet 4.2 in chapter 4) into the Methods section. Mention in this section that you have IRB approval or exemption.
What is your research question and hypothesis/purpose? Give a general idea of what you are doing and what you are about to explain:

2. Design: Talk about your design (e.g., pretest-posttest, one-shot, longitudinal, experimental, descriptive, or exploratory): how and when you collected the data, and what this design is supposed to answer. State the dependent variable (DV) and talk about how you are measuring it (O_1, O_2, O_3 etc.; the effect/criterion variables [IVs]; your program worked and made everybody better and happier and cured the world of social injustice). Tell what the independent variables are (X, the cause/the predictor: your intervention) and finally describe the characteristics and quasi-independent variables (don't forget demographic characteristics of your sample). Explain how you operationalized program objectives into measurable variables.
Is your design exploratory/explanatory/descriptive/quantitative and/or qualitative? What are the DV/IVs/pretest-posttest/operationalization method?

3. Procedure: This is for the procedures of your research study: who is doing what, how it will be done, the consent process, and when/where the survey will be given. Talk about how the intervention is run and if you will administer data collection before, during, and/or after the intervention.
Tell how you will get the data and how, when, and where you will evaluate the intervention. Include a brief descrip-

tion of the intervention itself and your procedure for acquiring it and analyzing it.

4. Sample: What is the N size (how many people you are collecting data on) and what are the ages of your sample? Describe who you are serving, eligibility/inclusion criteria, sampling methods (probability or non-probability, which is more likely for evaluation research). If individuals are not eligible for the study, then what are you providing them (referrals [to meet ethics requirements] or other services)?

Describe the sampling type and methods: probability (randomization)/one group or two/non-probability/sample size/eligibility for study/ethics/services for those excluded/ how and where you will recruit participants/eligibility or inclusion criteria.

5. Measurement: Tell how you are collecting data and with what instrument(s) (survey, interview, etc.); give reliability and if available validity scores (numbers such as $\alpha = ?$); describe the level of measurement for the instruments; and state whether these instruments have positive reputations, are fitting for the group under study, and are culturally appropriate. If you are designing your own instrument, describe it, talk about it being "piloted," and explain why you are creating a new instrument.

Data collection instrument/reliability and validity/culturally appropriate measurement/pilot? Describe the instrument.

6. Data Analysis Plan: Discuss the statistical tests you will conduct and why as well as what you want to show with

your numbers. If you will add a qualitative analysis, describe how you will code and increase the trustworthiness of the analysis. Will you use more than one evaluator for inter-rater reliability?

Quantitative (e.g., SPSS) or qualitative (e.g., NVivo/Atlas) data analysis? What are you looking for that might be statistically significant? How will you code for themes and patterns in textual data? For numbers, what statistical tests will you run?

7. Survey/Questionnaire/Measurement Instrument: Include the instrument you have created to collect your data.

PRACTICE EVALUATION: CASE-LEVEL DESIGN AS THE STEPPING STONE TO GROUP-LEVEL DESIGN

One way to lead those direct practice social work graduate students into the realm of group design is to use the single-subject or case-level design as the stepping stone to group-level design. Single-subject design is the therapeutic relationship measured at the individual level in a casework setting, a counseling session, or a case management interaction. It is the intake upon entrance to an intervention or the eligibility and assessment process for clients; it is the ever-present direct practitioner's one-on-one environment, and its sample size is $n = 1$. Combine a lot of single-subject designs, preferably $n > 25$, the smallest sample size for adequate evaluation, and you've got a group-level design, $n > 1$— magic! Nearly any agency intervention has some sort of measure on the individual level of treatment change and improvement.

There is your measurement, your data in the receptacle of an instrument, neatly packaged; collect more than one and you have a group-level design.

There are some things to keep in mind about single-subject case-level design. Although it is used in practice, was once popular, and is perhaps trending toward popularity again, it can change your program evaluation into a practice evaluation. It can be a very exact social science, and with those ABA designs (*A* is baseline measurement; *B* is intervention measurement) and the extinction, removal, or other status change of an intervention, it may be confusing to the student conducting a program evaluation. Although the single-subject case-level design is a building block and important as a guide to know how many singles equal a group, there are different rules for it. One requirement is the standardized instrument, which may not be very appropriate for program evaluation. Although a standardized instrument can evaluate client improvement, it may be best to conduct measurements using a more client-specific instrument rather than a treatment-specific instrument, such as those that measure how angry or depressed a person is. Standardized instrumentation is considered reliable and has the coefficients to prove it, but sometimes program evaluation is more concerned about how happy a client is in an intervention than about the scientific measure of the client's decreased depression. A great measure of an intervention for program evaluation, group-level design, is simply client satisfaction. Client satisfaction can even be measured as "I need more of this intervention." Worksheet 3.3 shows a perspective of single-subject practice evaluation as a building block to group-level program evaluation design. It also integrates contexts of client improvement under treatment, which is single-subject and the basis of all social work one-on-one interventions, with practitioner-based issues for use in direct practice.

Worksheet 3.3

PRACTICE EVALUATION

This is separate from the program evaluation, although it uses the same foundational research knowledge.

1. Describe the typical client who receives this program. Think of only one client, not the program, with an n size of 1. Give a profile of this person (gender, age, ethnicity, class, and position in life) and his or her reason for coming to this intervention and explain what makes him or her eligible for the intervention.

   _____

   _____

   _____

2. Explain how this intervention is intended to help the client; what is the intervention going to do for the client? Discuss the intervention and explain the theoretical basis and proven record (if this exists; if not, mention this).

   _____

   _____

   _____

3. Find a standardized instrument that will measure the baseline and intervention stages of program service delivery. Describe how success is measured (variables/coefficients).

   _____

   _____

   _____

4. Draw out a single-subject design (A = baseline, B = intervention).

   _____

   _____

   _____

5. To enhance this section (although not required), you are encouraged to add how you will gauge and enhance your practice wisdom and skills, such as continuing education, reflexivity, and consultation skills.

   _____

   _____

   _____

To conclude this "you can do it!" Methods section, think of it as a proposal of what you want to do in an evaluation. Think of the terminal question in evaluation—is the intervention working?—and go from there to design what is fitting for the data you have obtained from a social service agency. The data can be in any form: progress notes, pretests and posttests, or simply a database. Seek out secondary data because this is a more agency-directed approach for your evaluation, and you will avoid imposing some experimental method on your client. Put the elements together and then give them their research-y names, after the fact. For example, if you received 100 posttests from an agency, you have data and the instrument (posttest), and you have created a one-group cross-sectional design! If you have more than that, congratulations, you are fancy! But more than likely you will have a posttest single-group cross-sectional design: $X\ O_1$. Consider the single-subject as the $n = 1$ to your future $n = 100$ group-level evaluation. Get that IRB exemption so that you can become famous, or at least confident about your evaluation research, and then publish your advanced research course paper. Most importantly, remember that you are simply proposing this method and letting the agency direct you toward what it needs. Although you will want to impress agency staff with earth-shaking outcomes, you will provide them a useful product, earth-shaking or not. You are conducting social work research, empowering an agency, and helping it stay afloat with outcome analysis. This process in itself is divine, so be proud. And be ok with the way it all falls out. By all means, remember to brag to your friends and family about how you are conducting evaluation research!

METHODS TERMS

Group level: A study of a group of participants in the same intervention, a sample size greater than $n = 1$, in which the study is intended to measure treatment efficacy. Think of it as a group session being studied.

Case level: Also known as single-subject, sample size of $n = 1$, where treatment is measured along a baseline, followed by intervention (and sometimes changed intervention) and plotted in a graph. Think of it as an individual therapy session being studied.

Descriptive/correlational/quasi-experimental/pre-experimental: A mid-level research design that may have two groups, perhaps including a comparison group, and more than likely using non-probability sampling to describe and/or prepare for a more rigorous study.

Exploratory: A research design that is usually inductive and collects data on a case-by-case basis to explore or investigate an intervention using a more basic research method. This design may involve a large amount of qualitative data.

Explanatory: The most rigorous research method in which a theory is explained, or intervention or subject experimented on, with probability sampling and a control group.

Cross-sectional study: A slice in time; research done on a group receiving an intervention at one point in time, which can include both a pretest and a posttest.

Pretest and posttest: Data collection measurements that are given before an intervention is delivered and then again at the termination of an intervention. These instruments must be exactly the same to make appropriate comparisons of the before and after status of participants.

Independent variable (IV): The cause or an intervention. There are also quasi-independent variables that do not cause anything but are characteristics of a sample, such as demographic variables.

Dependent variable (DV): The effect or the observation of what has changed before and after an intervention is delivered.

Intervention: The independent variable, the assumed cause for a change in a participant after receiving it, and the primary subject of inquiry in program evaluation.

Operationalization: Taking a large, broad concept, such as happiness, and making it measurable by asking a series of questions that pertain to thoughts, beliefs, and behaviors related to that concept (e.g., smiling).

Sample size: The count of how many participants are in the study, represented by *n*.

Sampling techniques: Two techniques are used, probability and non-probability. Probability sampling is used for experimental research designs in which all possible participants have an equal chance of being selected; non-probability sampling fits with mid and lower level designs in which there is intention behind selecting certain participants in a given intervention and surveying them for improvements and feedback.

Purposive non-probability sampling: Sampling a group that is receiving an intervention intentionally, with purpose, for outcomes.

Randomization: In probability sampling techniques, after a sample is selected randomly (or by chance), participants are assigned by chance into one of two groups, an experimental group that receives a treatment and a control group that does not; then these groups are compared.

Secondary data: Data that have already been collected; also referred to as archival data. Data can be in the form of surveys, progress notes, intake forms, treatment plans, assessments, and anything pertaining to an intervention and the participant's interaction within that intervention.

Data analysis: An investigation of what numbers and words mean in relation to an intervention, either through statistical analysis or qualitative data analysis and coding.

Measurement: The recording of information in an organized way, such as writing down reactions to an intervention, giving a pretest before an intervention, or measuring the size of someone's foot.

Instrument: A designed document that directly records specific information that is relevant to a participant's satisfaction or improvement while in an intervention. Examples are a pretest or posttest, survey, interview, or poll.

4

Literature in Evaluation

AHHH, THE LITERATURE REVIEW—don't we all just hate it? The literature review can be the most bothersome, dreadful thing in an assignment, especially in research, because it can get so BIG. While walking down the literature review path, one can become quite lost, and thinking about the information presented may cause us to forget why we are here in the first place. There are some ways around the enormity of the literature review, as described in worksheet 4.2, "How to Do the Literature Review," which will be presented later in this chapter. The worksheet can be compressed even more to get the point across quickly, for example, by using only a couple of research studies and dropping the larger theory, but that depends on what is most fitting for the evaluation. If a larger framework is needed, this worksheet will work.

> *To use others' research effectively in your own literature review, comment on their evaluation design and sample (Methods), their findings (Results), and their implications (Discussion).*

In this chapter, two similar components of evaluation are combined, the literature or research review and the evaluation

the gooey Cadbury tinfoil-encased chocolate eggs that the bunny left on the fringes of your egg-hunting field. This is also known as starting wide in your literature review: grab it all and then start throwing out the not-so-relevant articles, keeping the ones you can use effectively in your research review. By the way, chocolate can make even a literature review fun. You deserve it; you're in graduate school or teaching research, and you should have a lot of chocolate! Worksheet 4.1 below will help shorten this hunting expedition.

Worksheet 4.1

READING RESEARCH TIPS

1. The title should tell you what you need to know (method, sample, and impact).
2. The title should be succinct but concentrated with information. When you skim a research article, start with the abstract and key words to search for the exact methodology, sample, or intervention, for example.
3. The first line/last line skimming technique usually holds true for research articles: you will find the purpose of the paragraph in the first sentence and the impact or point in the last sentence.
4. Search for words in headings, abstract, or content:
   a. *Quantitative*: hypothesis, bivariate or multivariate analysis, independent and dependent variables, literature review, theory, deductive, statistical analysis, any statistics tests named, random sampling and assignment, cluster sampling, simple random sampling, systematic sampling, probability sampling, explanatory, quasi-experimental (can also be exploratory), descriptive and correlational, pretest and posttest, larger sample size (bigger than 30-ish), internal and external validity, reliability coefficient,

operationalization, scientific objectivity, seeking truth, survey, questionnaires, closed-ended questions.
   b. *Qualitative*: purpose, smaller sample size (smaller than 30-ish), patterns, themes, coding, typologies, inter-rater reliability, inductive, exploratory, inductive, non-probability sampling, purposive sampling, convenience sampling, concepts and categories, naturalistic observation, anthropology, participant-observation, insider research, thick description, focus groups, social construction, seeking meaning, open-ended questions, interviews, first and second level coding, conceptualization.
   c. *Program evaluation*: quantitative and qualitative (can be both), logic model, outcome measures, intervention program, summative and formative evaluation, assessment, evaluability assessment, input, output, short-term and long-term outcomes, goals and objectives, social problems, client flow charts, benchmarking, consumer satisfaction, impact, process evaluation, cost-benefit.
   d. *Needs assessment*: quantitative and qualitative (can be both), target group, key informants, community members, secondary data, needs assessments and evaluation, identifying local needs, brainstorming, community, strategic planning, focus group, forums, organizational planning, surveys, resources, informational campaigns, gap in services, benefits, problem solving, assets, initiatives, polling, listening sessions, public input, asset mapping, eco-mapping.

When you search empirical research for introduction materials, use the following guide:

1. Abstract: need, purpose, hypotheses, design and method, sample, analysis, and findings with an implication or two.

2. Key words: primary words to alert the reader of topic, content, sample, and maybe method.
3. Introduction/literature review:
    a. First paragraph: establishes need or immediacy with statistics, trends, and overt statements of need.
    b. Body of introduction: begins broadly and progressively narrows to the hypothesis/purpose statement in the last paragraph; will present additional need for the research study and/or present theoretical bases buttressing the study.
    c. Last paragraph—the one the reader must attend to most—gives an overview of what is to come in the paper (sample, method, analyses, etc.) and most importantly the hypothesis (quantitative) or purpose (qualitative) the authors are testing.
4. Methods
    a. The who, what, and where.
    b. Skim the subsections: participants (sampling method), instruments (data collection method), and program/intervention.
5. For program evaluation, there should be a subsection explaining the intervention, and if it is not in the Methods section, it will be somewhere else in the paper (perhaps the introduction):
    a. Procedures (how they did the study, selection, and consent).
    b. Analyses (what tests/coding were used to arrive at the findings).
6. Results/findings: Don't start reading yet; go to the tables! This is where the data are presented.
7. Tables
    a. Quantitative
        (1) All numbers and this section speaks in statistics.

    (2) Tables should be in this order:
        (a) Demographics with averages and percentages, means, standard deviations, and proportions.
        (b) Correlations, Pearson and Spearman tests.
        (c) Non-parametric tests (chi square, Kruskal-Wallis, and Mann-Whitney).
        (d) Parametric tests (*t*-tests, ANOVA, and regression).
    (3) What is significant? What isn't? What are the variables?
  b. Qualitative
    (1) All text and speaks in quotes and words.
    (2) There can be a table of demographics, especially if mixed methods are used.

8. Subheadings: Skim subheadings for themes, patterns, and typologies for the findings with quotes used as data. Is it interesting? Do the themes make sense? Are they catchy?

9. Discussion/conclusion:
  a. The findings are translated so that the layperson can read and understand them.
  b. The primary findings, the most significant ones, are presented with discussion.
  c. Did the findings support the literature/theory?
  d. Did the findings support the hypotheses/purpose?
  e. This is the honesty section; what are the limitations? Self-critique.
  f. Implications
  g. What's next? What do we do with it? What does it mean?

10. References
  a. Check for name recognition (e.g., a reference by Freud would indicate psychoanalysis . . . a reference

by Saleeby would indicate strengths-perspective). These types of references are considered classic and can or should be used to establish theory.

b. Skim references to use for further search. Look for repeated authors or theoreticians.

c. Distinguish between the two main types of references:

   (1) References that support the research methodology used.

   (2) References that reflect two types of content: (a) statistics that show need and immediacy, and (b) literature that supports theory founding the study.

d. Method texts: Watch for these texts to help in deciding what the methodology is:

   (1) Quantitative: Shadish, Cook, & Campbell; Grinnell & Unrau.

   (2) Quantitative Statistics: Tabachnick & Fidell; DeVellis.

   (3) Qualitative: Padgett; Strauss & Corbin; Lincoln & Denzin; Alford.

   (4) Program evaluation: Weiss; Rossi, Freeman, & Lipsey.

   (5) Needs assessment: Alinski; The United Way (resource); Altschuld & Wilkin; Bryson; McKillip; Mintzberg.

   (6) Action research (needs assessment): Stringer; Greenwood & Levin.

   (7) Grounded theory: Strauss, post 1967.

   (8) Classic grounded theory: Glaser; Strauss when published with Glaser.

e. Political pieces:

   (1) Check the date the article was published; because it usually takes two years to get a submission finalized, data are probably at least

three years old already (you have to collect the data before writing the findings). The authors may tell you this on the first page.

(2) Check the university affiliation(s) of the author(s) and their disciplines (bottom of first page).

(3) Who funded the study (at the bottom of the first page or at the end of the content of the study)?

(4) Check the citation index for the journal (the higher the better; this is an impact rating); check the website and see what the journal says about its reputation.

(5) How many authors? All should contribute equally. The more authors perhaps the more technical the paper (a statistician, a theoretician, the graduate assistant, etc.). In medical journals, the last author is the primary author; for all others, the first author is primary author.

(6) What is the formatting? (For example, APA means that authors are social workers or psychologists; Vancouver is for sociologists, and so on.)

11. And a little more . . .

   a. Explanatory: purely quantitative methodology, all numbers, cause and effect, the gold standard, most rigid, experimental and control group, IV before the DV, randomization, controls thoroughly for threats to internal and external validity, the ideal experiment.

   b. Quasi-experimental or descriptive: purely quantitative, some controls for threats to internal and external validity, no control but a comparison group, not randomized, pretests and posttests.

   c. Exploratory: quantitative or qualitative, numbers or text, one group, one shot, maybe only one observation, no comparisons, non-probability sampling.

EVALUATION TIDBITS AND TERMS: ENHANCING THE LITERATURE REVIEW

There are pieces that need comment with reference to writing the literature review. Keep in mind the specific elements of program evaluation (and some elements can go into the Procedure subsection of your Methods section as well): formative and summative evaluations, needs assessments, process, efficiency, outcome and impact evaluations, and finally budgets and equations. Of primary importance in all evaluation terminology is a clear picture and description of the intervention under study; showing it graphically through a logic model is most helpful.

Integrating these elements, described in more detail below, into the literature review can make it more specific for readers and for those curious about how an evaluation works. It can also cut down on the fluff by narrowing the literature and research to what is specific to your evaluation. Your intention as a researcher of an intervention—investigating how the program is working—can be a formative evaluation to study how the intervention is flowing and growing, and to add efficiency, you apply the most basic equations for cost-benefit without subtracting the value of a person. By taking some liberties with the literature review in the evaluation context, you can provide a more reader friendly, creative, and useful presentation of ideas and research study. You can also show that you, as an evaluation researcher, are a friend, not a foe, as is commonly assumed about some external evaluators performing summative studies.

Formative and Summative Evaluation

Similar to all research terms, formative and summative evaluations are exactly what they say they are. *Formative* refers to forming or new; a formative evaluation is perhaps even a piloted program that comments on how a new intervention is going. A *summative* evaluation is a synopsis of an implemented program or intervention, and makes larger, more encompassing suggestions. The formative evaluation is the gentler of the two, focusing on feedback, input looping, and improvement. A summative evaluation is sometimes scary, with external evaluators submitting recommendations that can make or break an intervention. Formative evaluation needs someone on the inside to keep the process growing; summative evaluation may be assumed to involve an objective evaluator coming in and making much harder statements in administrative and delivery contexts. The trick would be to combine the two for an empowering and supportive evaluation process that does not intimidate those running a program and instead offers the evaluation researcher as a supportive and helpful ally and collaborator. This is the way to conduct evaluation; we have already established the need for social services and the oppression of social services, so why not be a helper instead of a scary monster?

If you are performing a formative evaluation, you should focus on how to improve feedback looping and collection of input from service providers, which requires research skills for pretest and posttest implementation, as well as for creating data management information systems for an agency and helping the agency grow by providing outcome measures that will support future grant submissions and funding. A summative evaluation has the same requirements as a formative evaluation; the one difference is that administrators should be given equal measures of positive and constructive feedback to enable them to decide what to do with said information. Again, this is a practice-based research model in which the practitioners decide the best course for delivery and implementation of the evaluation outcomes. Deciding what is best for your agency is better than being told what to do with your agency.

Needs Assessment, Process, Efficiency,
Outcome, and Impact Evaluations

Sometimes a needs assessment has been performed prior to the creation of an intervention, agency, or program. These are usually very large research studies, and when published, can offer only parts to be included in an article. They are great resources for establishing the need for an intervention, as well as for describing those who are in need of a social service. If you can find such a wonderful research study, use it for all it's worth. Additional program evaluation types can be described as follows:

- A process evaluation goes hand in hand with a formative evaluation because it investigates the workings of an intervention.

- An efficiency evaluation is usually about money, to determine whether it is being spent as intended and in an effective manner.

- Outcomes evaluations transpose on summative evaluations at times and focus on numbers of people served by an agency, improvement of a condition, numerical percentages of a target being reached, and statements that come in percentages of a whole.

- An impact evaluation focuses on the larger picture, such as how an intervention has cured the world of a particular problem, and how it has improved other realms outside the agency as well.

For more detailed explanations of these types of evaluations, see the glossary at the end of this chapter and review more detailed program evaluation texts referenced in appendix A.

The Easiest Formula for Efficiency Evaluation: Budgets

Social service agencies usually have public budgets, and if not, you can unobtrusively ask for these budgets in the context of an official evaluation. However, if a social service is hesitant to provide these numbers, do not press; it has enough entities to report to and is usually doing its own grant writing. To determine cost-benefit and cost-efficiency (see Grinnell, Gabor, & Unrau, 2012 for these differences), you can conduct a very simple cost-per-client estimate by dividing the total budget by the total number of clients served. This is a rough estimate and does not take into account the nuances, such as the costs of in-kind services, volunteers, and maybe even fundraising. But it does give an estimate. The more specific costs for an agency lie in the summative evaluation that is usually conducted by a funder, such as the state, city, or other entity providing funding. If you wish to be helpful to an agency in terms of budgetary evaluation, ask what staff would like to see and then request the budgetary data for these purposes. One issue with conducting cost-benefit and cost-efficiency analyses is the ethical question of whether quality of life can be reduced to a savings across time or if the worth of improvement can be calculated; it is tricky to quantify people and this sometimes reduces life quality to a mathematical equation. The safest and least threatening equation in budget analyses can be the simple expression of total cost of an intervention divided by number of clients served.

> *Total intervention cost/number of clients served = cost per client*

As an alternative for budgets and cost analyses in a program evaluation course, students can create a hypothetical budget for their evaluation services. Consider it this way: If the agency is your client and you are asking for an annual statement, even though you know the agency doesn't have much income, would you be insulting the agency by assessing its eligibility requirements? Keep in mind that these social service agencies are operating on small amounts of funding, and they are already accounting to multiple entities, including the IRS. If a budget analysis is not requested by the agency, do not force this financial analysis into efficiency evaluations. If the agency does request assistance with budgetary analyses, ask what staff wants to know and then apply very simple math, in frequencies and percentages, to provide the information that is needed.

Take into account and mention the different elements of program evaluation in your literature review; they are markers for comparison and contrast when you synthesize the research to your purposes. If requested by agencies, include budget and efficiency items. Outcome evaluation will provide the more conclusive numbers for promotion and future grant funding.

The Intervention and Logic Models

In the literature review, it is important to promote, explain, and even sell the intervention. The literature review is really about the intervention, and all information needs to relate to this intervention in demonstrating relevance, edification, and research synthesis. A great way to reveal the intervention is through a logic model—a graphic representation of the intervention including inputs, outputs, impacts, resources, and objectives (see the Research Resources in appendix A for logic model templates). The logic model nicely transposes onto the evaluation types, including outcomes and impacts. Figure 4.1 shows what goes into the intervention, called *inputs* (e.g., people, intervention materials, office space, and clients). In the middle are outputs, which are the objec-

FIGURE 4.1 LOGIC MODEL

tives met in an intervention delivery, the intervention itself, the statistics of those served, and overall numbers that show that the intervention is reaching the target population effectively. At the end are impacts that, similar to impact evaluations, show the larger, wider picture of what the intervention intends to accomplish, such as to end world hunger.

INTERVENTION OBJECTIVES: YOUR OPERATIONALIZED MEASUREMENT

When you describe the intervention in the literature review, think of it as the precursor to measurement. Every agency and intervention has a mission, goals, and a series of objectives. These objectives are the measurable goals that are integrated into a research study. There must be something measured in order to report outcomes. For example, if an objective is to assist clients with housing, this objective will need to be expressed in numbers, such as "Agency X will reach 75 percent of the targeted population in area X over the duration of a year to link X number of families to stable housing." These objectives can be found in treatment plans, in the data mining process, in progress notes, in percentages and frequencies kept by the agency, and in other outcome data. It is the evaluator's job to locate these data and compile them into organized and summarized statistics for outcome reporting. These objectives can also be measured in the pretest and posttest. For example, the pretest might ask if a client has housing, the dependent variable's first observation. Then the intervention is applied, possibly as case management (the independent variable) to locate stable housing. After the intervention, the posttest will determine if the client has housing at this point, the dependent variable's second observation. A great way to remember how to make objectives measurable is the SMART model (Doran, 1981), shown in figure 4.2. Although this model is exceptionally useful in program development, it can also be used in measurement and even in incorporating the programmatic evaluation (integrating outcome measurement and feedback looping) into an existing intervention, which would be the helpful and empowering way to deliver program evaluation. In this manner, a researcher can create mechanisms for the agency to use for future funding, effectiveness, and promotion of the social service.

S	SPECIFIC
M	MEASURABLE
A	ATTAINABLE
R	REALISTIC
T	TIMELY

FIGURE 4.2 SMART CHART

This model also helps the researcher to measure outcomes for program evaluation. These measurable objectives are exactly what you are converting into numeric data to convey to others, in the form of percentages, charts, tables, and pictures, that the intervention is effective; it is working because it is meeting and maybe even surpassing these objectives.

THE LITERATURE, THEORY, NEED, AND HOW YOU'LL MAKE IT ALL BETTER

Worksheet 4.2 below will walk you through a somewhat traditional format of the literature review in a step-by-step process. As you read through it, always keep the intervention in mind. Remember that this is being written for an evaluation—an outcome report—and be sure to consider whether all items have spoken to these ends. This will keep you on track. Use only the literature, research studies, and statistics that you need; keep the literature review as exact, concise, and to the point as possible. No fluff, just the facts; that is research.

Select the research studies that you need to support your evaluation purposes, such as similar interventions, program evaluations, and other literature that addresses the larger picture of what is under study (e.g., the topic area, population, or even the intervention type itself). Synthesize the research studies, using the findings, methods, and implications to support your intervention and your evaluation of it. For theory, locate the larger, broader theoretical framework that founds the intervention. For example, if you are evaluating an intervention that addresses social skills, consider finding a larger theory of education. If you are evaluating drug and alcohol rehabilitation, consider finding theory surrounding rehabilitation. To grab the reader's attention, usually in the first paragraph, cite the service need and social statistics of the social need. For example, use federal census numbers to address the need for housing or food distribution and the incidence and prevalence rates of HIV/AIDS or mental illness. Federal databases and other Internet sources can provide the social need statistics that will reveal to your reader the essential nature of the intervention, as well as the need for the evaluation to show its essential outcomes. Finally, in most literature and research reviews, your conclusion will reveal the need for your evaluation, the need to publish it and share the information, the edification provided by the intervention, effective outcomes, and its contribution to the knowledge base. With your evaluation, you can address the need and show the method of investigation in a very excellent way, and thus make it all better with your contribution.

Worksheet 4.2

HOW TO DO THE LITERATURE REVIEW

Purpose of the Introduction/Literature Review: This section of the literature review is intended to introduce your reader to the program intervention you are evaluating, including the history and theory behind it. The standard research question for a program evaluation is to ask if the program being delivered is effective, has effective outcomes, is financially feasible, is being implemented as intended, and is essentially showing a change in the recipients from pre-intervention (pretest) to post-intervention (posttest). Start broadly and then narrow your focus to the final paragraph that will reiterate and clarify why you are conducting this external program evaluation, the need for it, your hypothesis (quantitative) or purpose (qualitative)—how you will show the program is needed and all about the program intervention—and finally what you are going to do next (and segue into the next section, Methods). As a hired/contracted evaluator, be sure to refer to whoever is conducting this program evaluation (for example, this program evaluation is being funded by the Casey Foundation and contracted with the external firm of The Best Evaluation Ever Group to fulfill state and federal requirements for outcome evaluation).

Requirements: You must locate, read, and cite at least five research articles in this section that include (a) the statistics on the need and prevalence of the population being served, (b) the theory behind the intervention program, and (c) other studies of the program intervention (research studies about your program intervention). You may need to refer to a textbook for the theory piece.

1. Grab your reader's attention with statistics showing the need within the population you are serving with your program intervention; show in statistics why your evaluation is urgent and timely.

   _____

   _____

   _____

2. Talk about the big theory or theories behind your program intervention. (There should be one; your intervention will be much more credible if it is founded in theory.)

   _____

   _____

   _____

3. Talk about what other people have done with this same or a similar intervention, critique how they did it, and finally describe how your program evaluation study builds on their knowledge, adds quality information, and provides much needed improvement (again, how your study will rock).

   _____

   _____

   _____

4. Be sure to describe what the intervention is and does and how it rocks. Tell about mission, goals, anticipated outcomes, and purpose of the intervention. It is essential to mention and discuss a logic model of the inter-

vention program here (include a completed copy in the appendix). It is also essential to mention and discuss the budget (expenses, funding, and costs of the program); include a complete copy in the appendix.

_____

_____

_____

5. End with an overall reminder of what you're doing and why, the research question, and what is next (Methods). You can move or rearrange the above sections to increase flow and clarity, but always end with the summary/reminder paragraph.

_____

_____

_____

To conclude, although the literature review appears to be a daunting task, you can make it efficient and meet your needs with some slight alterations, such as synthesizing, not annotating, the existing research. Use all items of information in this section to edify the intervention under study as well as to show that your evaluation is sound, the methods exact, and the results important. Focus on the evaluation terminology to keep your study in the evaluation realm of research, and thereby narrow its perspective. Let the statistics that reveal need for the intervention do the talking for you. Save your energy for the more important sections, which are Results and Discussion. And finally, don't be ashamed of your dorkiness if you get into the research; embrace it, be proud, and proclaim that research is sexy!

LITERATURE AND EVALUATION TERMS

Formative evaluation: A mid-level research design that investigates the process of an intervention, sometimes at the beginning of intervention implementation; integrates feedback looping; and focuses on improvements and enhancements of delivery.

Summative evaluation: An evaluation type that is broader in scope than the formative evaluation and makes decisive recommendations, based on outcomes, for correcting or sometimes ending certain elements of intervention delivery.

Needs assessment: A large, exploratory research study that measures preliminary needs of a population or areas surrounding a social need to establish a standard for intervention delivery to alleviate these needs.

Process evaluation: A research study that parallels formative evaluation and focuses on the delivery of an intervention and studies the flow, implementation, and arising issues in the implementation.

Efficiency evaluation: An evaluation type that studies cost and budgetary issues, assesses whether an intervention is delivering what it claims, and is aimed at minimizing delivery costs.

Outcome evaluation: An evaluation type that focuses on the statistics of delivering a service, including the population and number of clients served and the percentages of needs that are addressed.

Impact evaluation: An evaluation type that focuses on broader, far-range results of service delivery, such as alleviating a social need and measuring benefits to society.

Logic model: A graphic representation that integrates action into service delivery, showing resources as inputs into the intervention, midpoints of services as outputs, and the impacts of the intervention on the greater good, such as the alleviation of a social need.

Fidelity: An evaluation standard that refers to the integrity of service delivery; if the evaluation continues once auditing is complete, a term that indicates whether a program or agency has integrated evaluation into its process and delivers the intervention as prescribed.

Utility: An evaluation standard that refers to the usefulness of a program evaluation.

5 Data Management: Between Methods and Results

THE SPACE BETWEEN DESIGNING YOUR methodology and running statistics or coding qualitative data is when the real work happens. This is the time for putting your methods into action. As you do so, you may see some changes in the methods as your agency coordinator sends you in new directions to provide the agency with meaningful materials and outcomes. When working with secondary data, you must determine, sometimes with little or no information, just what the variables represent, and this can be challenging. For example, you may need to clarify definitions of variables (e.g., if a variable called number in household really includes all persons in the household).

An agency may request that new data be collected, which requires the creation of a survey or interview-type questions and a solid purpose behind this new data collection instrument. Because some smaller agencies do not have pretests and posttests in place, it is extremely helpful to have an objective and research-directed person create these instruments to assist in outcome reporting. Instrument design is a very important reporting tool; it can provide follow-up information on how participants are improving and document their status after they receive an intervention. There are many options, not only in designing practice research, but also, depending on the amount of time allotted, in converting a research project into a feedback looping process that can establish an unobtrusive and ongoing data collection system and data management with analysis conduit for the agency. You can create a living research project for the agency to ensure timely and easy delivery of outcome measurement and reporting—magnificent!

OPTIONS FOR DELIVERING THE CONTENT

The author delivers her graduate-level advanced research course, called Practice and Program Evaluation, over the course of a semester. Secondary data and descriptive statistics are about as sexy as this research can be when conducted over the limited time of a single semester. Although students can pull off a simple survey and some data collection within a semester, the process is usually rushed, and hindsight is the operating condition of such evaluation measurement. A secondary data analysis with one group can be effectively conducted in a single semester, even with additional time allotted for figuring out the intervention and the data. The author currently has students working toward publication of their work from this one-semester research study so this compressed time frame can lead to big things! A one-semester project establishes relationships and collaborations with the instructor and agency that can be revisited for future study.

If the instructor and students have options to work together across sequential semesters, then there is time for a more in-depth design, original and new data collection, piloting newly created surveys tailored to the agency's needs, and IRB approval. By extending the time for research study beyond the one-semester course, students and their instructors/mentors can build an applied research study that turns into a thesis, dissertation, publications, and even grant submissions.

With the skills you have gained from method and design, this in-between place within evaluation research offers you the opportunity to design a bigger and better study, one that can propel itself when you walk away from it, especially if you have the time to extend the research over more than one semester. As you are looking at data, entering data, and maybe even collecting data, those thoughts you have about how to improve the design are building blocks for a better design: write down those thoughts and ideas! As you enter data, create a better database; as you read surveys, create a more comprehensive one; as you analyze data and wish you had interval/ratio levels of measurement, write the survey questions in this format. These thoughts are stepping stones to building a better research study and one that is more effective for practice settings to show their outcomes and actions. Your evaluation ideas about the research in front of you can even lead to grant writing, future funding, and increased access to services within the field setting of your study. Table 5.1 delineates possible options with suggested time frames.

The steps for a one-semester secondary evaluation research study are included in this manual. Sequential two-semester and longer studies can utilize elements in this book as a foundation, and will be covered in more detail in the following pages.

Whatever the time frame and options for course-based research studies, there are essential elements for the one-on-one interaction between instructor and student, and these can be labor intensive. The author normally offers students whom she works with over a semester the opportunity to work with her again in an independent/directed study to continue their work, which would lend itself to a two-semester research option. Even if students do not take additional courses, the author always offers to help them publish their work after the course. Many students' advanced research projects then become an ongoing learning process that can be expanded and refined over time. Additionally, with more than two semesters, these students may become doctoral students, and the work they began in their simple semester-long MSW research course can grow into an applied research dissertation.

TABLE 5.1 STUDENT, INSTRUCTOR, AND AGENCY RESEARCH TIMING OPTIONS

Time frame	One semester	Two sequential semesters	2+ sequential semesters
	Design and product options		
Method	One group, cross-sectional, posttests	Newly created administered surveys, pretests and posttests, possible two-group comparison design	Longitudinal pretests and posttests, two-group comparison design
IRB	Exemption	Exemption or approval preferred	Approval
Instrumentation	Pre-collected pretests, archival documentation	Piloted surveys, agency-tailored surveys and/or interviews	Surveys and interviews tailored to agency needs, piloted in the second semester
Data	Secondary, quantitative/ minimal qualitative	New data, quantitative and qualitative equally	Secondary and new data, mixed methods, additional qualitative data collection
Analysis	Descriptive, correlations, chi-square, with some coding patterns	Descriptive statistics through t-tests, increased qualitative coding with exploratory investigation for piloted surveys	Descriptive statistics, t-tests, and regressions for predictive models; typology creation from qualitative patterns
End product	Course paper; grant materials	Manuscript for publication; written grant proposal	Thesis/dissertation; submitted grant proposal

The instructor can answer varying degrees of research questions according to his or her teaching philosophy, which in this manual involves a mentorship role. For example, if students need more hands-on terminology, the instructor will adapt the mentorship to this role; if students have achieved more applied research methods, mentorship can be more hands off. If the instructor's school curriculum allows it, students can extend research opportunities over a longer period of time, and this may even result in a new niche for both instructor and student.

ORIGINAL RESEARCH

When you work with social service agencies and conduct evaluation research with them, the opportunity to truly tailor your study to their practice needs is a very wonderful thing. Agency-directed, practice-based research conducted in field settings can both empower and secure essential social services through outcome assessment and reporting, and you can be the person who built this resource for the agency! When you conduct original research for an agency, similar to secondary data analysis, your initial priority is to be with this agency—learn about its intervention, how it conducts business, what data are available, and what the agency wants to learn about its programming; we could call this *sitting in the agency* or learning about its life situation. Consider what the agency is interested in and what it has access to, and think of yourself as a researcher in the field and with the field. Always remember that what you are doing is for the agency within its practice. You are using your exceptional research skills to assist the agency in areas where the needed resources may not be available, such as evaluation; you are providing a unique gift because you are creating research methods that are specifically tailored to agency needs.

The agency will inform you of its current data resources and its needs; many agencies simply need survey instrumentation to collect data that reveal outcomes. Knowing methods and design, including how to measure variables, puts you at an advantage because this knowledge can help you create the best measurement for the agency's intervention. Remember that pretests and posttests are the most effective measures to show changes in attitudes, knowledge, and skills and that the pretest and posttest must be exactly the same. Considering how the agency delivers the intervention helps you to unobtrusively measure baseline knowledge, for example, and assess subsequent changes in a posttest. These surveys can be administered at intake and again at exit from services, during a case management meeting or counseling session. Rapid assessment instrumentation is best because it is quick, requires minimal effort to conduct, and can be easily integrated into intake assessment as well. Consider consent and always inform participants of your intentions and purpose with regard to their feedback. Consider conducting interviews as a means to develop and pilot surveys and outcome measurement, as well as to provide participants time to express their needs and wants within an intervention. An interview can feel like a counseling session if it is done correctly, and it is always a compliment to ask someone for input. A comparison group may also be effective; this can be accomplished by simply having like participants complete pretests and posttests. If the agency is providing more than one intervention, participants can be selected through comparative matching.

As outlined in table 5.2, there are many options for original research that can be quite simple. In fact, the original research process can be completed in six steps: (1) create collaboration with an agency, (2) determine the data in existence and the data needed, (3) ask the agency what outcomes it wants to measure, (4) create a survey based on agency directives, (5) administer the piloted survey to participants in the intervention, and (6) analyze and share the findings. This effort can be an ongoing research experience over sequential semesters if both instructor and student agree.

Establish the connection with an agency contact and get the go-ahead for an ongoing research effort; the agency is more than

TABLE 5.2 ORIGINAL RESEARCH STEPS IN PRACTICE SETTINGS

Step	Task
1	Partner with an agency for evaluation research.
2	Determine existing data.
3	Determine needed data as directed by the agency.
4	Create a survey based on the needed data; test it on fellow students, friends, and family; and make changes for aesthetics and readability.
5	Purposively sample all available intervention recipients to pilot the new survey; administer the survey.
6	Create a data management system for the survey that can include secondary data and/or additional demographic data.
7	Enter data, analyze data in SPSS, and compile the results in report form; integrate graphics and/or outcome pamphlets.
8	Share with the agency, preferably in a formal and group setting.
Two sequential semesters	Add to the research recipe: 9: IRB approval for future publication 10: A comparison group 11: Interviews to expand/improve survey.
More than two sequential semesters	Add: 12: Regression analysis for predictive models 13: Increase qualitative interviews/data for typology 14: Grant elements and possible grant submission.

likely to agree to ongoing research because this research will be an exceptional benefit for outcomes reporting and it will be free. Yes, conducting your own original research within a practice setting can be as easy as conducting secondary research, as you will see below. It may even be more helpful to the agency because it creates a more permanent solution for outcome reporting that is uniquely tailored to their needs.

RESEARCH IN THE FIELD: THE SETTING

There is a definitive setting for practice-based and agency-directed evaluation research. This setting contains three parties: student, instructor, and agency liaison, and research can be conducted in a variety of formats. It does require a proximate, intimate mentoring relationship between the student and instructor. The author has somehow managed to set up such a mentoring environment with a large class of more than 30 graduate students. This larger class requires a division of class time into content delivery, followed by individual meetings with groups. The practice evaluation requires student and instructor interaction and talking with social workers in the field, exposure of students to social work field settings, and openness on the part of the instructor to learning and adaptation from academia to practice while working within an applied research context. This is a negotiated research and practice field evaluation collaboration.

Some suggestions for increasing the efficacy of the setting interaction are to invite field instructors to an inclusive preemptive meeting with students and the instructor. Elements to address are what exactly the students will be doing and how the research process will help each party mutually. For agencies this help lies in the outcomes; for students it is the experiential learning. Ultimately it will become the student's responsibility to negotiate and interact, within this setting, with the data and with the research agenda while integrating practice-based and agency-directed mandates of the evaluation research. Presentations from students to agencies after the conclusion of their assignments are most beneficial for student learning and foster pride in their work. Presentations are beneficial to the agency because the information is shared with multiple stakeholders.

There are many formats for the initial interactions that introduce evaluation research collaborations. The most appropriate format depends on the social work school's contacts, the instructor's contacts, and student contacts. The author has established research relationships in the field in two ways: (1) by asking students to go out and solicit these collaborations on their own and (2) by garnering partnerships with local social service agencies before the course starts. Both methods have benefits and can be adapted or combined as needed. Students and agency partners do need to know that students will spend some time within the field setting collecting data, entering data, and organizing data and that they will interact with agency staff to clear up any issues or questions. The process of analyzing and compiling results for write-up, including design and methods issues, will most likely occur within the classroom and lab as guided by the instructor. The primary element of this research study being conducted within the field setting is that students will gain immense knowledge simply through their exposure to the practice setting as well as behind the lines in data collection, analysis, and outcome report writing.

REFLECTIVE RESEARCHERS:
ALL THIS THINKING IS HURTING MY HEAD

As mentioned previously, between methods and results is the real work; it is important to reassure students that this work can be compartmentalized and that any requests for new data collection can be addressed with simple effort, requiring only a basic knowledge of how to ask a question and how to put numbers into an Excel spreadsheet. This knowledge is founded on the idea of the reflective researcher (for more information, see Peake and Epstein

[2004] and any writing by both authors on practice-based research). The reflexive researcher is a researcher, or evaluator, who can look back, or reflect, on what data he or she has and how to make sense of them; put them to good use; and transform them into outcomes, materials for future grant funding, and products that an agency can use for fidelity in its intervention delivery, as well as for measurement of intervention efficacy. As a reflexive researcher, the author engages in life-long learning and reflexive practice, meaning that research is integrated into practice, and she continues learning through practice experience as well as through formal routes. The reflexive researcher seeks understanding, knowledge, and improvements through work experience and practice-based research.

The reflexive researcher who inhabits this space between methods and results may think quite a bit about how best to manage and analyze the data. This is not necessarily a comfortable place for students, who will be thinking about how best to measure an intervention, how to code data, and how to figure out the research of this evaluation thing. There has been a transition—from trusting the process and being patient to wondering what to do with the numbers and words acquired and thus reflecting on the most effective evaluation process for an agency. This reflection is truly helpful and very agency-directed because it is for the benefit of the agency. The reflexive researcher will soon make sense of it all. What is consoling at this point in a semester evaluation is that now the hands-on experiential work begins. This doing of research usually requires students to reflect on the process thus far and what is next; questions begin to arise for students that are applied research learning moments.

Practice-based research is a component of reflexive research in that the evaluation is an inductive process, meaning that the agency director says "this is what I need to show." Living and operating within this social service guide the research questions that need answers, or outcome promotion, and require access to existing data. Students can provide the reflective component by saying "If I could design the perfect evaluation for Agency X, I would integrate aftercare measurement." The practitioner provides the knowledge of what data are collected and what he or she needs to show; these are the research questions the students in turn can inductively ask to show the agency's outcomes. The reflexive researcher is the one who is saying "Oh, yeah, I get that!" and "It would be really cool if they measured this . . . ." When you're getting it, and the process is creating more questions than answers in your head, then you have become the research geek and reflexive researcher; congratulations!

ALL THINGS DATA

Now that you have the data, in whatever form, it is time to organize them for upcoming data analysis. To run statistics on quantitative data, the data must first be organized and transformed into codes. The qualitative coding will be explained in detail at the end of this chapter. You may even have more qualitative than quantitative data; this is great because qualitative data can be used to explore in-depth meaning more effectively than quantitative data, and they can be useful for survey development. Qualitative data provide guidance on how an agency may need to measure outcomes. Remember, even your ideas and thoughts about this process can be used as data. These ideas (field notes or memos) are qualitative data that can be used for evaluation and programmatic improvements, as well as for survey and scale development.

> *Nominal and ordinal data require* **codes** *or labels to be run in SPSS. Codes are simply numbered labels; they are not real numbers.*

Data Management

Organizing data means putting on paper, and in a spreadsheet, all the jumbled mess of ideas and numbers given to you (and in your head) in a more comprehensible format. First, the secondary data acquired need to go into an Excel spreadsheet. Some agencies already have spreadsheets or a database for collected data; some do not. The spreadsheet is essential to organize the data; it is what we call a data management system, or a management information system. Whatever you call it, it is the recording of data for future outcome reporting. Many agencies do not have statistical software such as SPSS, and hence Excel is needed to run outcomes. Excel does have some nice computational capacities, but not as many as SPSS; this is where a school of social work can help with the outcome analysis. Your university should have license to use SPSS. Data management is simply creating a place to put the data for future outcome reporting.

There is a step-by-step process that can help with this in-between place of hands-on and experiential work in program evaluation:

1. Acquire secondary data (quantitative and/or qualitative) or collect new data from a new measurement.
2. Design a code book. As the measurement is the instrument used to collect data, such as a pretest, the code book defines the variables in the instrument with the levels of measurement for each variable, such as name or grade.
3. Define variables (operationalize them) based on the data collected and the code book. Variables are the questions asked (for example, variable = male or female?).
4. Code nominal and ordinal variables (examples: 1 = male, 2 = female; 1 = *strongly disagree*, 2 = *disagree*, 3 = *agree*, 4 = *strongly agree*).

5. Using your code book, enter the data into Excel: data entry should mirror that used for SPSS for ease in copying Excel data into SPSS.
6. Check your work. One way to do this is simply to look at the spreadsheet and seek out patterns; look for items that do not match these patterns.
7. Transition your Excel spreadsheet (for the agency) to an SPSS database (to run outcomes). With SPSS, there are two page tabs per database: data view and variable view:
   a. Variable view:
      (1) Define variables: string (qualitative) or numeric (quantitative).
      (2) Set limits on decimals and characters.
      (3) Add a descriptive label.
      (4) Add values, which are your codes for the levels of measurement.
      (5) Determine if nominal, ordinal, or scale (interval/ratio) level of measurement is appropriate.
   b. Data view:
      (1) Copy and paste the data from Excel into SPSS.
      (2) Do this in parts at first, and slowly, to check your work.
      (3) Copying and pasting into SPSS will show you if you defined the variable correctly; if you did not, the data will not paste.
      (4) Check your work. An easy way is to simply look at the database and see if there are blank spaces or extraneous numbers that fall outside of the coding range.

Database Design

Database design is creating an Excel spreadsheet that reflects the measurement that collects the data, meaning that it is the piece of paper on which a participant has answered *agree* or *disagree* to a question you asked. A variable is the question itself (e.g., what is your gender?). Enter such a variable along the top row of the spreadsheet and give it a name (e.g., gender). Then on the column below the variable, enter the answer as coded: in this case, 1 for male or 2 for female. The code must be entered to make it easier for you to copy and then paste into SPSS. Although SPSS cannot run statistics on the term male, it can run statistics on 1 by organizing all the 1's into percentages, modes, and ranges. Your database should have as many variables as there are questions on the instrument, such as a pretest, and maybe even more if you have created new variables, such as a composite pretest score for all pretest answers. To create composite variables, simply run a median or mode statistic on all answers from one participant, and put this new code into a new variable column that is specific to the participant. Rows in Excel are for the individual responses of one participant. The columns along the top are for the variables or questions on the instrument.

The Excel database will look very much like the SPSS database, if not exactly the same. The SPSS database has an additional page view, the variable view that Excel does not have. This view is used to show how a variable is coded, provide label descriptions of a variable, and define whether it is a nominal, ordinal, or scale (interval/ratio) level of measurement. Remember, a database is simply the organized receptacle for data. All it does is organize and hold the data for future outcome analysis and reporting.

Data Entry

Entering the coded answers into your fancy database takes some time; the learning curve should be steep at first because you are getting comfortable with the codes and maybe re-familiarizing yourself with the ten key (love the ten key!) and checking to ensure that you are entering responses as you coded them. Enter *999* for any missing data; this is to remove said data from the statistics run when we get to the SPSS database. Database entry may require no work at all if the agency has given you its database (jackpot!); it may take some time if the agency has handed you a pile of unorganized pretests and posttests (still, jackpot!). In the latter case, organize the pretest and posttest by participant before you begin your data entry. Start slowly to get comfortable with data entry; as you progress, you will find that you are doing it in your sleep. A great way to check your work is to (1) leave the data and return later, requiring you to find your place when you return; (2) enter the data from last answer to first; and (3) after you enter a case, simply use your finger to follow the answers entered in Excel as you look through the instrument.

Coding and Code Books

Again, in data entry all coding is based on the levels of a variable that you have defined; it is the number that corresponds to a name you have given a variable so that SPSS can think about it in a numerical sense. For example, a question on the pretest is "Do you love research?" The answer choices are *very much so* and *sort of*. This variable (Do you love research?) is coded on two levels: 1 = *very much so* and 2 = *sort of*. Codes 1 and 2 are labels given to the responses to a question. That is all coding means in data entry and database creation. You will need a guide to be sure that you don't enter 3 = *hate it* because this was not an answer option.

> *The word **code** in research can mean many things: a label assigned to a nominal or ordinal variable, a way to document patterns and themes in qualitative data, and a secret password to gain access into the research geek clubhouse.*

The easiest code book is a copy of the measurement with lovely marked-up colors used to define the codes in the margin by the question. Keep your code book beside you as you enter data and copy it into SPSS. For example, copy a blank, unanswered pretest and write your codes in the margins next to every question. In red, beside the question Gender?, write 1 = male, 2 = female, and refer to it often as you enter the data. The code book is a great guide to ensure that your data entry is on track. You can print a code book from SPSS after you have created the entire variable view as well.

All Things Are Data

A comprehensive spreadsheet, a thank you note, a daily service log, a pretest and a posttest, an exit survey, a demographic sheet, a progress note, and counts of how many persons were served—these are all data. And all these items can be entered into Excel and SPSS. Just remember to define a string (word) variable and a numeric (number and code) variable when you enter or copy your data into SPSS. Although SPSS cannot run statistics on qualitative data, it will give you a list of the answers in a format that is more organized and contained for your analysis. You can also use qualitative software programs to help in text coding and analysis, but that instruction is for another textbook. We will talk more about qualitative coding below.

> *"All is data."*
> *Barney Glaser*

Your thoughts, ideas, and noticed patterns in data are data as well; make a note of these for future writing in your Discussion section. You can even analyze your thoughts and ideas into trends and patterns for inclusion in the Results section. These ideas that you have about the data and intervention are very important in the direction of evaluation and strengths-based outcome reporting and in helping an agency streamline its assessment process.

THE QUICK SURVEY: SURVEY IN A SEMESTER

So what to do if the agency asks you to create a pretest and posttest? Or if the agency requests a follow-up measure for participants who have left the intervention? These are the perfect creative products to give an agency for its own evaluative process, and this survey development can be fun and simple as well. First, remember that the agency needs these types of measurements to show effective outcomes; hence, you should create these surveys according to agency needs. With this information, use your own creativity to design an aesthetically pleasing instrument that is easy to complete and captures the needed data in a simple way. For example, questions on a pretest need to be the same as those on the posttest because you want to compare apples to apples. A one-page questionnaire is sufficient for many interventions and it is less intimidating to the participant. You want to ask both closed-ended (quantitative) and open-ended (qualitative) questions of the participant. You can ask very simple questions—such as "Would you refer a friend to this agency?" and/or "Did the intervention help you?"—because, at this point in the research study, you know the intervention very well and can ask these questions with a foundational knowledge of what needs to be reported in an outcome assessment.

Consider, when you design an agency-directed survey, how you would ask anyone a question and provide choices for response (e.g., yes or no or even maybe), and allow participants a chance to give even more information as an explanation of why they did or did not like an intervention. For example, "On a scale from 1 to 10, 10 being highest, how much did this intervention help you?" or "How has the intervention helped you since leaving the program?" Yes, again, it is that simple. Keep in mind that the pretest and posttest are the best way to go and that they need to be unobtrusive as well as edifying to participants. This means that participants will feel good about completing these surveys and that you have considered the easiest and most convenient time for a participant to complete them. Use basic and easy-to-read language, and keep questions concise and specific. Short and sweet is a nice mantra for instrument design. Your survey creation may be administered by someone in the agency who is overwhelmed, running the entire show, and has little time to do such a thing as data collection.

> **Survey** *usually refers to a quantitative measurement, such as a pretest and posttest.* **Interview** *usually refers to a qualitative, open-ended data collection tool.*

There are some items, such as threats and how to control for these threats, that you should keep in mind when you design instruments for new data collection. These threats have to do with validity of an evaluation research study—is the instrument used for data collection truly measuring the efficacy of an intervention? There are many ways to address these threats and to keep your simple and easy instrument design and evaluation study valid. You should also consider the reliability of the instrument—is it a precise and an effective tool? Ways to control for such reliability and validity threats are listed in worksheet 5.1; the most common in program evaluation tend to be piloting instruments as well as piloting interventions.

Worksheet 5.1

CONTROLS FOR THREATS TO VALIDITY (COZBY, 2007)

1. Controls for threats to reliability
   a. Pilot the instrument
   b. Obtain participant feedback
   c. Test-retest
   d. Use alternate forms
   e. Split-half (comparison of differing versions of a survey)
   f. Internal consistency (Cronbach's alpha)
2. Controls for threats to validity: you can generalize outside your sample only if you have used random selection and random assignment
   a. Random selection
   b. Random assignment with control group
   c. Time order of IV before DV: manipulation of IV, relationship between IV and DV
   d. Pilot study
   e. Participant feedback and debriefing
   f. Deception (when participants do not know the purpose of the study)
   g. Filler items (for survey development or checking)
   h. Placebo groups
   i. Field setting and observational research
3. Controlling for researcher bias
   a. Training
   b. Run conditions simultaneously

    c. Automated procedures

    d. Double-blind experiments

    e. Manipulation checks (IV has the intended effect?)

4. Threats to internal (cause and effect) validity: the independent variable did not actually cause the dependent variable

    a. History

    b. Maturation

    c. Testing

    d. Selection bias

    e. Mortality

    f. Regression

5. Threats to external (generalization) validity: you cannot generalize outside of your sample

    a. Multiple treatment interference

    b. Researcher bias

    c. Pretest treatment interaction

    d. Reactive effects

    e. Selection treatment effects (you did not conduct random selection and random assignment)

Piloting measurements and trying things out ahead of time are controls for instrumentation threats; whenever you create a new measurement for an agency, call it a *pilot*. This will imply that changes can easily be made and adjustments to questions integrated as participants complete the survey or questionnaire. This is another feedback loop; it can coordinate both agency-level and participant-level input into improvement in measurement and reveal outcomes with ease and grace.

Data collection, when directed by an agency, can also be combined with the agency's secondary data and compiled into a primary database and data management system. Another accessible and helpful tool for data collection and instrumentation piloting is Survey Monkey. This online software is free for short surveys, is easy to create, and collects data in Excel. If you need a larger instrument with more features, it is economical as well, and if you are conducting a larger study, you can purchase a one-year license for SPSS import capacities. There are many software surveys out there, but none, in the author's opinion, are as easy and cost-effective as Survey Monkey. Another suggestion for survey design and data collection is to develop both a hard copy and online electronic survey. This can meet the needs of persons who are less Internet-savvy, and it will address more comprehensive coverage in sample size for all persons involved with an agency intervention. Worksheet 5.2 below will provide some ideas on developing surveys for program evaluation. Creativity and appeal are essential elements that will make the survey your creation and product and ensure effective outcome measurement for an agency.

Worksheet 5.2

SELF-REPORTS AND SURVEY DESIGN

1. List the goals for the intervention:

   _____

   _____

   _____

2. List the specific services offered in the intervention:

   _____

   _____

   _____

3. What does the agency delivering the intervention want to achieve from it?

_____

_____

_____

4. What would a successful client for the intervention look like?

_____

_____

_____

5. Now write down what you want to know about your clients:

_____

_____

_____

6. List the questions you want to ask:

_____

_____

_____

7. How will you ask these questions?

_____

_____

_____

8. What type of scale will you use? What are the levels of measurement?

   _____

   _____

   _____

9. Are you basing this scale on another scale? Yes or No

10. How are you going to improve the scale?

    _____

    _____

    _____

11. What measurement questions would be relevant for the program and what measurement questions would be relevant for the practice?

    Program: _____

    Practice: _____

12. What are the reliability (the scale is good) and validity (it measures what it says it does) issues?

    Reliability _____

    Validity _____

13. Design your survey below, including the questions you want to ask:

QUALITATIVE IS A NECESSARY ABUNDANCE: SORTING THE DETAILS INTO COMPREHENSIBLE MATTER

"How did the intervention help you?" is a qualitative, open-ended question that allows a participant to answer in words or narrative. Qualitative responses are usually obtained from interviews and fit the exploratory design method best. Qualitative data are simply words. They can be explanations, follow-up questions, or feedback that needs coding and description after analysis. In pre-experimental methods, qualitative data are usually a complement to, not the primary focus of, a series of more specific quantitative questions. In acquiring secondary data from agencies, you may find you have a lot of qualitative data, and you may be unsure what to do with them. Think quality when it comes to words. This quality will provide in-depth and meaningful explanations of any quantitative elements in an evaluation. Qualitative data are a great way to explore an intervention, and if you are creating a new pretest and posttest for an agency, add open-ended questions that can later be transitioned to quantitative forced responses for more rapid assessment instruments. If you are creating a scale, your method definitely needs to be exploratory; you definitely need qualitative questions.

> *Index cards are a great way to assess where students are in the semester. They are also a great way to demonstrate qualitative coding.*

Do keep in mind that qualitative data analysis takes more time and that it is more laborious for participants and researcher alike. Additionally, these textual questions need much thought and focus behind them to avoid having them become too daunting for a person to answer. They need to be simple and answerable. Coding qualitative data requires thought and creativity, as well as an ability to read between the lines. It also takes up more space in a Results section because quotes, not numbers, are the data that serve as evidence for your interpreted codes, and numbers take up less space.

Qualitative coding is a lot like quantitative and statistical analysis; both types of data need sorting and organizing. With quantitative data, you are organizing numbers via statistics and describing what they are in ways that summarize and present the data in a way that our minds can process them. Qualitative coding refers to the manner in which a researcher looks at the words, finds the comments and ideas that repeat, sorts them into categories, delineates them to form patterns, and then expresses them in a different way that is more accessible to a reader. What makes qualitative data accessible is the researcher's effort to find themes and patterns, apply names and labels, and then show the support (quotes) for these themes and patterns.

Qualitative coding can be easy if you let it be. It is a heuristic process, meaning that participants are telling you something, but they are modest and do not understand how great this thing is that they are telling you about. It is up to you, reflexive researcher, to name this great thing. That is the heuristic process—collecting qualitative data and then naming the thing it represents for the participants. This means that the participants don't know exactly what it is they are doing; it is your job to find it and name it. The main steps for qualitative coding are laid out below, followed by worksheet 5.3, which describes qualitative methods and how to walk through a qualitative study:

1. Take the text data, separate them from the numerical data, and organize them.
2. Read once, superficially, through all the data, noting the ideas that emerge. Have paper and pen ready . . . .
3. For first-level coding, read all answers for questions 1, 2, 3, and so on. Write down the recurring responses to the specific questions.

4. For second-level coding, read more deeply into the responses across all answers, not just for certain questions, but for the questions as a whole, looking for conceptual ideas, such as "displeased with intervention because wanted more time in the intervention" or "gratitude for the intervention."

5. Organize first- and second-level coding separately, keeping notable quotes (ones you want to highlight) organized by putting them into a table, a flow chart, or into graphics that show a process.

Worksheet 5.3

HOW TO DO QUALITATIVE METHODS

1. Grounded Theory (Classic/Orthodox/Glaserian)

   About: Considered a general method, grounded theory (GT) can be used with qualitative or quantitative data. Theory generated is grounded in a group's observable experiences. It develops with no initial hypothesis, describes what happens, and explains why the phenomenon occurs based on observation. It begins as an inductive process, followed by deductive reasoning, which is used for sampling. It is dynamic: what the researcher starts out with may not be what he or she ends up with. The five components are theoretical sensitivity, theoretical sampling, coding, theoretical memoing, and sorting. The main focus is discovering how a group resolves a basic social process. It is based on the issues of the participants; it is totally participant-driven.

   Requirements: An initial sample of 4 to 5 persons (which can grow into 20 or more), field notebook/journal, colored index cards, sorting system materials, and an open mind.

Method: The GT researcher usually teaches herself or himself how to conduct this method (what Glaser calls *minus mentorees*) and as such learns while doing. The idea is to trust that data conceptualization will lead the researcher to where she or he needs to go next. Quotes are not used because GT is based on conceptualization; the researcher captures the thought and imagination of readers by generating/ interpreting codes from the data. Theoretical sampling determines the sample, which may change as the researcher seeks out diverse participants to gain insight into core codes. Interviews are conducted via *adjusted conversational interviewing techniques*, meaning that the researcher asks a main question and then adapts to the interviewee as he or she deems necessary. Method and analysis are inseparable in GT. The researcher does an interview and then compares content immediately. This is called the *constant comparative method*.

Analysis: Analysis and data collection occur simultaneously. The researcher seeks out the core code in the data through *open coding*, or coding the data in every possible way. When the core code is discovered, then selective coding occurs: selectively coding for a core variable. This leads to the theoretical codes for write-up. The researcher always stops field note transcription when an idea, concept, or revelation emerges from the data (memoing). The researcher will have many ideas about the data and he or she will record them because they are the basis of the memo. He or she will seek the core code, or basic social process, and its resolution. All data relate to this code in some way. When interviews are complete, the researcher will begin sorting through the memos and placing them in relevant categories. This is when a literature review occurs, the opportunity to research theory that relates to the core code. (Note that the researcher does not do a literature review before developing the method because this could lead to forcing preconceived ideas onto the data, which may be incorrect.) The researcher then begins the write-up phase of the GT process.

End Product: A discovered/generated/created theory based on the basic social processes of participants.

Example: The study of how lesbians survive culture that is exclusionary.

Resources: Anything by Barney Glaser, Sociology Press, Mill Valley, CA, http://www.sociologypress.com/.

2. Ethnography

About: The long-term investigation of a group, culture, or society that is based on immersion and participation in that group; a detailed exploration of a group. It employs multiple methods to arrive at a theoretically comprehensive understanding. The issue for the observer is how the particulars in a given situation are interrelated. The focus is to describe and interpret a group or culture and how it operates in its natural environment.

Requirements: Acceptance into a group; established trust and rapport within the group; recording materials such as field journal, tape or digital recorder; video camera; still or digital camera; and lots of time.

Method: Many formats are used for data collection, but immersion into the group is primary; the researcher is a participant and therefore issues may arise, such as reactivity of the group to the researcher and prolonged engagement to reduce bias. Observation and interviews are used and supplemented with artifacts. Steps are as follows: (1) description of the group (behaviors, activities, norms, values, etc.), (2) analysis of these components, and (3) interpretation of these components for write-up. An observational protocol will need to be developed so that the researcher can focus on primary data collection and not feel the need to collect all data, which is a distraction. Information can be stored via field notes, recordings, or computer files, for example.

Analysis: The researcher organizes files for the data and reads through the material, making notes to find codes in the data. Descriptions of the social setting and events and even pictures are used to analyze and interpret the data. The researcher then classifies data according to themes and patterns. After managing the data, reading and memoing the data, describing the data, and classifying the data, the researcher interprets the data and makes sense of the findings. Finally, the researcher represents and visualizes the data for others to understand by giving a narrative presentation.

End Product: Possibly a book or extensive articles on cultural norms that may be supplemented with visual data collection; a deeper and culturally laden understanding and/or interpretation of a group's processes, values, and issues that is very detailed and comprehensive.

Example: Study of health care settings and cultural parameters that may affect a population's response to care.

Resources: Ethnographies are mostly within the domain of sociology/anthropology; many books can be found in these disciplines about ethnography, including one by M. Craig and L. Cook, *Doing ethnographies* (Thousand Oaks, CA: Sage, 2007).

3. Practice-Based Research

About: Used with both qualitative and quantitative methods, this process begins as an inductive process that originates from a specific practice-based issue. It can be very useful in social service settings where funding has been cut and the agency must prove efficacious service delivery. The researcher uses what there is already without seeking out more data; the client chart is the jackpot. The study is unobtrusive, pragmatic, and cost efficient. It also requires a reflexive researcher, meaning that the researcher has insight into a need, has information about the population, and has tacit knowledge about the political nature of the environment. The researcher is able to look back into previous issues, readdress them, and seek out current understandings with what is available.

Requirements: A reflexive practitioner, client charts, agency and client need, perhaps support from administrators, and extra time to spend with the charts.

Method: As qualitative analysis, this process begins inductively from practice wisdom. The researcher should investigate chart material that is textual and record descriptive and correlational information. This can be done in collaboration with others to direct the exploration of the charts and definition of what the researcher is seeking. The researcher does a literature review and researches program evaluations to direct this exploration. She or he should survey all available information sources (intakes, progress notes, etc.). Once it is located, information must be strained before its value can be determined. This may be only a preliminary exploration because the findings may only lead to more questions and barriers.

Analysis:

1. Locate a site and determine what information is available to analyze.
2. Assess the credibility and legibility of notes.
3. Determine the unit of analysis.
4. Perform a literature review to conceptualize concepts and modes of analysis.
5. Inventory the variables found in progress notes and handwritten correspondence.

6. Develop forms that can be used to extract information from the charts.
7. Select a sample of charts depending on the key characteristics.
8. Begin directed sampling using data extraction forms to collect data.
9. Analyze data, code, and make interpretations.
10. Write up the information in a report that practitioners, auditors, and administrators can understand.

End Product: Problem identification, barrier discovery, evidence of successful research completion by practitioners, cost benefits, enhancement of service delivery.

Example: Establishing an identified need that hinders service delivery and is unmet by community mental health programs that can be used to lobby for additional funding or reallocation of current resources.

Resources: See, for example, I. Epstein and S. Blumenfield, *Clinical data-mining in practice-based research: Social work in hospital settings* (Binghamton, NY: Haworth, 2001).

4. Focus Groups

About: Although they are not always the final product in qualitative research, focus groups can be used to direct and formulate purpose statements regarding a topic area. They can be self-contained as the primary source of data and they can be used as a supplementary source of data or for multi-method studies. A group of people is brought together to talk about their lives and experiences in a free-flowing, open-ended discussion that usually focuses on a single topic. Focus groups are a rapid method for collecting data. They are considered useful with marginalized populations, they are empowering, and they have an action orientation. Participants automatically compare their experiences to provide insight into the topic.

Requirements: Six to twelve persons and as many groups as are willing to discuss the topic of interest; tape or digital recorder; paper and pens; and perhaps two researchers, one to record interactions and the other to facilitate the group.

Method: The facilitator opens the discussion with all participants. Having two facilitators can reduce distraction. To minimize bias as opposed to seeking generalizability, purposively select the sample. Groups must be composed of like persons for free-flowing discussion. Determine the level of structure and involvement from the moderator. Determine the group size, number of groups, and interview content and create a protocol. Choose a neutral and convenient site for data collection.

Analysis: There are essentially two units of analysis, the content of the discussion and the interaction dynamics in the group; the art is to balance these two in the analysis. Begin coding after transcription has been finalized. Coding involves (1) all mentions of a given code, (2) whether each participant mentioned a given code, and (3) whether each group's discussion contained a given code. Examine one or two groups for detail about these codes; then apply them across the groups. Interpret the codes. The researcher decides at this point which topics, codes, and themes will go into the final report. The write-up will include direct quotes to support themes and interpretations of codes.

End Product: Research data in and of itself, or data that can direct future semi-structured qualitative interviews, quantitative survey research, and mixed methods. This is a great way to pilot newly created quantitative surveys.

Example: A group of women come together to discuss barriers in the workplace.

Resources: See, for example, D. L. Morgan, *Focus groups as qualitative research* (Thousand Oaks, CA: Sage, 1997).

5. Life Histories/Narratives

About: Although not one and the same, life histories and narratives are built on the same pretext: participants sharing their stories. Life histories may be more structured and focus on one process in the participant's life. Narratives may be more open-ended with participants defining the focus as they tell their stories. Narrative and life histories are studies into ways participants experience the world. Narratives can be broadly focused, whereas life histories, or short-term observational studies, can be more narrowly focused on specified categories of group behaviors.

Requirements: A group or person of interest who informs the topic of interest, time to allow for complete stories and perhaps follow-up, tape or digital recorder, a field note journal, and a sample willing to share their stories.

Method: Field notes, interviews, journals, letters, autobiographies, and oral stories are methods of narrative inquiry. If you are seeking out specific topics, develop a semi-structured guide, adding probes for prompting. Rapport will need to be established with participants. Explain the researcher's role in the interview. In a sense, this method is similar to adjusted conversational interviewing, in which the researcher modifies the interview tactics as needed for the participant's comfort and disclosure. Decide on what the unit of analysis is, whether it is a specific topic and you seek out the sample (life history/short-term study), a specific group and its unique experiences (narratives), or a single person (biography). Decide whether to use new interviews or existing data (archival or secondary research).

Analysis: Similar to other methods of qualitative research, the primary analysis lies in the coding and interpretation of the categories. *Microanalysis* (line-by-line reading to flesh out categories), also called first-level coding, is the first step, defining core issues, categories, and properties.

Developing a coding system for organization is primary. After coding and comparison of codes, second-level coding occurs. This involves deriving the purpose, interpretation, meaning, and explanation of the patterned themes. Finally, the write-up requires definition of the codes, quotes to support the categorization, and your interpretation of the quotes.

End Product: A deeper, more emotive understanding of a person; group of persons; or a specific topic unique to a group of individuals. This product can be used to direct quantitative study.

Example: Study of how academic women experience their university environment through many formats such as journals, free-flowing storytelling, writing, and semi-structured interviews.

Resources: See, for example, R. Atkinson, *The life story interview* (Thousand Oaks, CA: Sage, 1998) and D. J. Clandinin, *Handbook of narrative inquiry* (Thousand Oaks, CA: Sage, 2007).

6. Action Research

About: Community-based action research is a collaborative approach to inquiry and investigation that provides people with the means to take systematic action to resolve specific problems. The unit of analysis is the problem. This approach to research favors consensual and participatory procedures that enable people to (a) systematically investigate their problems and issues, (b) formulate powerful and sophisticated accounts of their situations, and (c) devise plans to deal with these problems and issues. Action research is totally participant-driven, empowering, and change-based.

Requirements: Groups willing to become active, involved, and open about recent problems and issues in whatever area they operate. There must be investment by all stakeholders in the process due to the collaborative nature of action research and the intensive work involved. This may require money and support and will definitely require time, in addition to materials needed for smaller scale qualitative endeavors.

Method: The basic routine of action research involves (1) looking (gathering data, defining the problem, and describing it), (2) thinking (analyzing and theorizing), and (3) acting (planning, implementation, and evaluation). The researcher is a catalyst and may be affected by the problem. He or she first assesses the problem and then creates consensus and negotiates the outcome. Preliminary activities involve establishing contact, identifying stakeholders and key people, establishing the researcher role, and constructing a preliminary picture of the research plan. The researcher then facilitates consensus on the new vision and begins collecting data through interviews, observation, and existing documents. Meetings with stakeholders and participants throughout the data collection phase are essential.

Analysis: This method is similar to other qualitative methods, but there is an added feature beyond simple reporting of the study results: the final analysis lies in action. Action research involves three steps of analysis and write-up: (1) selecting key features of experiences and then categorizing them; (2) representing participants' voices and needs through reports, ethnographies, and biographies that are expressed in written form or through such media as drama, dance, poetry, or song; and (3) action, involving the procedures, plans, projects, services, programs, and policies to be implemented and/or changed. Effective write-up and marketing of the research requires innovation and creative expression as well as the standard published article.

End Product: Political change and consciousness raising, as well as the required "publish or perish" research articles and creation of a network and collaborative community.

Example: University women collaborate with other campus groups and researchers to address the problem of unequal pay in academia.

Resources: See, for example, E. T. Stringer, *Action research*, 2nd ed. (Thousand Oaks, CA: Sage, 1999).

QUALITATIVE METHODS TERMS: TRANSPOSING TECHNIQUES AND BASIC CONCEPTS AND FOUNDATIONS AND PARADIGMS

General

Inductive: From case to theory (qualitative method); building on specific observations to make inferences and generalized statements.

Deductive: From theory to case (quantitative method); conclusion about a specific case based on the assumption characteristics are shared with entire class of similar cases.

Data Collection

Open-ended questions: Unstructured questions; response categories are not fixed.

Interviews: Data collection in the form of words; participant responds not to numerical categories but to self-report of experience.

Semi-structured interviews: Interviews that are open-ended, but have specific topic information to guide responses and probe into deeper answers.

Saturation: The point at which no new themes emerge in interviews and the researcher begins to hear the same content repeatedly; the time to stop the interview.

Naturalistic observation: Recording data as they occur under natural conditions.

Analysis

Transcription: A written, printed, or typed copy of interview data or any other written material used in data analysis.

NVivo: A software program that, among other features, allows the researcher to import qualitative interviews that can be coded, modeled, and summarized.

Dragon Naturally Speaking: A software program that will take digital voice recordings and transcribe them automatically into an electronic document.

Microanalysis: First-level coding; line-by-line reading of text to generate initial categories.

Coding: Thematic, overarching patterns sought out in the text of the interviews.

First-level coding: Initial coding to identify meaning units, fit them into categories, and assign codes to the categories; the coding foundation; microanalysis.

Second-level coding: Higher level coding; a more abstract interpretation of what first-level coding categories mean and imply.

The Sample

Key informants: A subpopulation of research participants who are knowledgeable about the research topic and have access to other potential participants.

Snowball sampling: A common qualitative technique in which study participants refer other similar or different participants for sampling; useful for divergent views.

Sample size: Unlike quantitative research that uses larger sample sizes, qualitative methods can collect sufficient data from fewer participants, ranging from 15 to 40 persons.

Strategies

Insider researcher: An argument in qualitative methods that the researcher is a best fit when he or she shares similarities with the group under study. This assures access, rapport, and tacit knowledge.

Validity: In qualitative methods, credibility, truthfulness, and reality in findings.

Inter-rater reliability: The degree to which multiple raters/ coders find the same results.

RESEARCH PLAN OUTLINE FOR QUALITATIVE METHODS

Note that the research plan outline is different in classic grounded theory:

1. Proposal development and IRB approval must occur first, but your method and purpose are well formulated and designed by this point. It is better to ask permission, not forgiveness, when conducting research. If your research is not approved, you cannot publish it and to do so would be an ethical violation.
2. Research topic
   a. Introduce the study.
   b. Present the problem and need.
   c. Introduce the purpose of the study.
3. Literature review
   a. Present current issues, research, and theory.
   b. Describe how your study is similar to and different from other studies.

    c. Explain how your study fits with others.

    d. Conceptualize the variables to be used in your study.

4. Conceptual framework (how concepts are connected and linked to theory)
5. Questions and purposes
6. Operationalize definitions
   a. How will you measure the variables?
   b. You can condense sections 2 through 6 and also combine them.
7. Research design (one group, sampling types, pretest and posttest, longitudinal, etc.)
8. Population and sample
   a. Purposive, non-probability sampling.
   b. A general description of participants.
9. Data collection (a detailed account of how data are collected, from whom, what data, and when)
10. Analysis and findings (discuss findings using quotes and conceptualized codes)
11. Discussion and conclusion
    a. What do the findings mean and what are their implications?
    b. Limitations of your study.
    c. Future research implications.

The space between the methods and results requires a lot of work, and this work entails database creation, data entry, perhaps some survey design, and coding and code book creation. It is necessary in program evaluation to give credence to the processes of compiling, organizing, entering, and analyzing data for what is written into an outcome report because this is where a lot of the thinking takes place, as well as problem solving and creation. At this juncture, you should be seeing the fruition of your hard work and problem solving, evidenced in a database and data management system.

DATA MANAGEMENT TERMS

Excel: A Microsoft program that organizes and summarizes numbers and data within a spreadsheet and that can be used to present data in the form of tables, charts, and graphs.

SPSS: The Statistical Package for the Social Sciences, a software program that allows the user to enter, organize, and summarize data through statistical tests, with tables, charts, and graphs.

Coding: The process of labeling levels of a variable with numerical tags or ranks in order to conduct statistics; the process of analyzing qualitative data into named patterns and themes.

Codes: The number or rank assigned to levels of a quantitative variable; the labeled or named titles in qualitative data that represent an issue, theme, or pattern.

Range: The upper and lower numbers of a spectrum of numbers; the minimum and maximum response categories in a grouping of a single variable.

Levels of measurement: How response items are coded to represent the varying degrees of answer choices, such as nominal (name) or ordinal (ranking) answers; also real numbers that are divisible such as interval and ratio variables (age and/or temperature).

Threats and controls: Threats are issues that may make a measurement less than what it can be and may interfere with the results. External threats are outside influences that confound the ability to generalize outside a sample and internal threats are inside influences in testing that confound the causative effect of the intervention on participant status.

Heuristic process: A process that occurs when surveying and studying a group, the participants' answers are embedded with possible theoretical implications that when taken alone may be difficult to discover, but when combined are easy to uncover; the individual may not know that such implications and processes are occurring.

6 Results

WHAT YOU HAVE NOW IS a mess of numbers and words, and although they are organized in Excel spreadsheets and SPSS databases, they are undecipherable to anyone other than you. At this point, you should have a very effective working knowledge of the data and variables; if not, go back to the measurement and ensure that you understand the levels of measurement for each variable. Write down the thoughts that you have about these variables while you consider the main research question: is the intervention effective? You may notice that you do not have enough information to answer this question so consider other interesting elements of the data, such as what participants look like, their demographic information, and other possible evolving questions whose answers are just waiting for you to break them out from within this mess of numbers and words.

What the next step must be then is to put this information into a format that others can read; this will require some, but not a lot, of statistical knowledge that is presented below in worksheet 6.1. There are three operations that fit well with program evaluation when running statistics on quantitative data: (1) descriptive statistics and frequencies, which reveal percentages, counts, and measures of central tendency; (2) correlations, which show associations and relationships among variables; and (3) hypothesis tests, which investigate interesting findings from items (1) and (2). It is more than likely that you do not have the rigorousness of an experimental research project and not so many, if any, interval/ratio levels of measurement. Hence, although you cannot truly do *hypothesis testing*, you do want to investigate findings from your frequencies and correlations by using additional tests, such as chi-square, *t*-tests, and even logistic regression.

For example, an interesting issue you may encounter after running a correlation is that there is a statistically significant finding and the correlation coefficient is negative. Hmmm. This means that, while one of the variables goes up, the other goes down, which is an inverse or negative relationship. However, the bivariate correlation test does not say which variable goes up while the other goes down, and a follow-up test is needed, such as a chi-square for nominal or ordinal variables. The chi-square will report percentages and proportions that show which variable becomes greater while the other becomes less.

> *If you are feeling overwhelmed by all these numbers, walk away for a bit. Fresh eyes help, as does a break. The numbers aren't going anywhere, as long as you have saved the database in a couple of places. You'll really want to walk away if you lose your data, although for some, like your professors, this is a rite of passage in program evaluation.*

To better prepare you for reading those pages and pages of SPSS output after you run some statistical tests, not quite sure of what it is you are doing, the statistical tip sheet (worksheet 6.1) can help you in answering some of those lingering questions. This sheet can help you navigate the statistical syntax and commands for the Results section, and show you how to present these findings in narrative, charted, graphic, and tabular form.

Worksheet 6.1

STATISTICS HELP SHEET

Variables

Dependent variable (DV): A variable that is dependent on, or caused by, another variable. The outcome variable is not manipulated directly, but is measured to determine if the independent variable had an effect. Simplest term: the effect. It is your main variable of observation, and statistical tests are determined on the level of measurement of the dependent variable. You can have more than one DV or multivariate stats (multiple variables). Multivariate stats also imply that you are examining more variables than just the relationship between two variables (bivariate). One variable is univariate.

Independent variable (IV): A variable that is not dependent on another variable, but is believed to cause or determine changes in the dependent variable; an antecedent variable that is directly manipulated to assess its effect on the DV. It does not have to be manipulated (nonexperimental research, quasi-independent variable). Simply put, this is the cause. You can have many IVs, and you will usually have more than one. Additional variables may be participants' variables (gender, ethnicity, etc.) that are important to analyze, but cannot be manipulated.

A variable: The characteristic or quality that describes a measured concept, behavior, attitude, characteristic, for example; the quality that makes the variable measurable. Variables are defined in four attributes (levels of measurement): nominal, ordinal, interval, and ratio.

Levels of Measurement (see table 6.1)

Nominal: The most basic measurement. Attributes are mutually exclusive (one or the other, not both), categorical, naming only one class or category (male/female).

Ordinal: The next level up. Attributes are mutually exclusive, categorical, and rank ordered; they are different but cannot be measured quantitatively. Commonly used are Likert scales (1 = *strongly disagree*, 2 = *disagree*, 3 = *neutral*, 4 = *agree*, 5 = *strongly agree*).

Interval: The next level up. Attributes are mutually exclusive, rank ordered, continuous, and equidistant from each other. You can quantitatively measure the difference between scores (getting ten words correct on a vocabulary test is twice as much as getting five correct).

Ratio: The highest level. Attributes are mutually exclusive, rank ordered, continuous, equidistant from each other, and have a true, absolute zero point (for example, income has an absolute zero: I made $0 one year and $2 the next).

Interval and ratio scales: In SPSS, there is no difference between interval and ratio scales; they are used in the same manner. The difference between interval and ratio can be tricky in social sciences; if you make a 0 on that vocabulary test, it does not necessarily mean that you didn't take the test or that you have no vocabulary ability.

TABLE 6.1 STATISTICS HELP SHEET: LEVELS OF MEASUREMENT

Level	Different categories/ mutually exclusive	Ranked	Distance measured between categories	True zero	Attribute	Example
Nominal	Yes				Categorical	Gender
Ordinal	Yes	Yes			Categorical	Likert
Interval	Yes	Yes	Yes		Continuous	IQ test
Ratio	Yes	Yes	Yes	Yes	Continuous	Income

Statistics (see tables 6.2 and 6.3)

Descriptive statistics: Summarize, organize, and describe data via frequency distributions, percentages, central tendency (means), and variability (standard deviation).

Inferential statistics: Using sample statistics to infer findings about the population; generalizing back to the population from sample findings. Based on chance or probability of error (p); the smaller the probability of error, the better. Accepted levels are $p < .01$ (1 in 100) and $p < .05$ (5 in 100).

Statistics that determine association: chi-square, χ^2, and correlation, r (Pearson for interval/ratio levels of measurement (LOM) and Spearman for nominal/ordinal).

Statistics that determine differences: independent and dependent t-tests.

Reading statistical tables: Look for those asterisks (*); they will provide a p level ($p < .01$, $p < .05$, etc.) at which the statistical test was significant, showing little error due to chance, or that the significance/difference is not coincidental.

The order of things: When you read journal articles and quantitative research (statistics is about quantitative research; the numbers give it away), APA format dictates what data are presented and in what order they are presented in tables, starting with descriptive statistics and working up to higher levels or inferential statistics used to test the hypothesis. Some of the descriptive statistics may be omitted from the journal due to space limitations. Sometimes these tables are combined (descriptive and inferential stats together). Tables should reveal, in this order:

1. A description of the sample giving central tendency (means, medians, and modes) and variability (standard deviation and range), as well as frequencies and percentages (chi-squares and t-tests may also be presented early).

TABLE 6.2 STATISTICS TESTS

Statistics test	DV (1 only)	IVs	IVs	Example (DV first, then IVs)	Statements
Chi-square (χ^2)	Nominal	Nominal (1)		Gender (M/F) and grad degree (Y/N)?	Associations
Spearman correlation (rs)	Nominal/ordinal	Nominal/ordinal		Gender (M/F) and income (low/middle/high)?	Relationships/ associations
Pearson correlation (r)	Interval/ratio	Interval/ratio		Age and income (interval)?	Relationships/ associations
Logistic regression ($\hat{Y}$, χ^2, R^2, OR)	Nominal	Nominal/ordinal	Interval/ratio (not essential)	Gender (M/F), income (low/middle/high) and age?	Associations/ prediction/ relationships/ odds ratios
Multiple regression ($\hat{Y}$, R^2)	Interval/ratio	Interval/ratio (2+)	Nominal/ordinal	Income (interval), years of education, and gender (M/F)?	Associations/ predictions/ relationships
t-tests, independent (t)	Interval/ratio	Nominal/ordinal		Income (interval) and gender (M/F)?	Differences/ group mean comparisons
t-tests, dependent (t)	Interval/ratio	Nominal/ordinal		Pretest/posttest scores and gender (M/F)?	Differences/ group mean comparisons
ANOVA, one way (F)	Interval/ratio	Nominal/ordinal (3+ levels of IV)		Test scores (interval) and income (low/middle/high)?	Differences/ group mean comparisons/ effects
ANOVA, two way (no. of IVs = no. of ways; F)	Interval/ratio	Nominal/ordinal (2+ IVs)		Income (interval) and gender (M/F) and income (low/middle/high)?	Differences/ group mean comparisons/ effects
ANCOVA (no. of IVs = no. of ways; F)	Interval/ratio	Nominal/ordinal	With covariate interval/ratio	Income (interval) and gender (M/F) and covariate age	Differences/ group mean comparisons/ effects

2. Relationships between variables. These are correlations, if needed for certain tests such as regressions (Spearman and Pearson).
3. Next, the fancy stuff to test hypotheses. If you have categorical data for the DV, then you will see chi-square and logistic regression. If you have interval data for

TABLE 6.3 PARAMETRIC AND NON-PARAMETRIC TESTS

Parametric statistical tests	Non-parametric statistical tests
Assume normal distribution	No assumption for normal distribution
Larger sample size	Can have smaller sample
More statistical power	Less statistical power
More generalizable	Less generalizable
Continuous variable (interval/ratio)	Categorical variable (nominal/ordinal)
Fancier stats tests (ANOVA)	Not so fancy tests (chi-square)
Differences	Associations

the DV, then you will see *t*-tests, ANOVA/ANCOVA, and multiple regression.

Ordinal levels of measurement: This is tricky . . . both nominal and ordinal intervals are categorical. What can be problematic with the above mentioned statistical tests is when the ordinal scales have many categories or attributes (more than three), making it hard to interpret the output from SPSS. With an ordinal scale that has many attributes/levels, use special tests for ordinal data:

- Mann-Whitney U-Test: An alternative to the independent-measures *t*-test.

- Wilcoxon Signed-Ranks Test: An alternative to the repeated-measures *t*-test.

- Kruskal-Wallis Test: An alternative to the independent-measures ANOVA.

> *When you read SPSS output, look for the asterisks. They denote statistical significance (p), meaning that the coefficient is so different that something very different among the numbers is occurring, with error factored in. One * is a p level equal to or less than .05; two ** is a p level equal to or less than .01. This means error is so small that something big is happening in the numbers.*

SPSS, READING OUTPUT, AND STATISTICS IN A PURIST MANNER

Keeping it as simple as possible when running your statistics is essential; this helps convey your findings to those "non-research-y" folk who need your outcomes for grant submission and reporting. You aren't out to impress anyone with your mathematical skills; you just need to be credible and show understanding of the statistics you have run. However, your newly found mathematical skills are a bonus as a social worker so drop this tidbit about you in job interviews; you have practical statistical knowledge now! Learn just enough to complete a useful evaluation, and thus not confuse the findings with fanciful numbers that no one understands. Percents and counts convey valuable information for outcome reporting, and funders, as well as you, understand percentages and counts. So remember: (1) counts, (2) relationships, and (3) follow-up tests on a couple of interesting findings, such as large numbers of a specific group and negative relationships between group characteristics and attitudes in (1) and (2). And never run a mean on a nominal or ordinal variable (see the statistics help sheet, worksheet 6.1). This is a very common error that no one likes to talk about. A great example is student evaluation of teaching and instructors, usually measured on a Likert scale. Results for professors are then presented as averages, and this is incorrect. The median should be reported because ordinal variables are not real numbers, and although the rank is known, it is not divisible. Run a median or mode as a measure of central tendency for Likert-scaled item responses.

Here's what the Results section is: (1) running the statistical tests; (2) reading the SPSS output; (3) writing the output into technically laden and APA formatted sentences that convey the findings; and (4) creating charts, tables, and graphics that summarize these statistics for those who prefer pictures to words. And that is it! Run the stats, figure out the findings, write about the interesting ones while integrating the terms and numbers in a uniform format, and then provide pictures and tables to simplify these findings. Although this section sounds daunting, it can all be created using guides and APA sentence structure. You simply plug in the numbers and present an occasional thought with them. This section, needless to say, is full of numbers, symbols, subheadings, and tables. And for the most part, the only difference between the Results sections across many articles is the numbers presented in them, which are unique to the research program evaluation study. If you have qualitative data and results to present, put these findings after the quantitative ones. Create tables and graphics for these findings as well. Grants commonly require quantitative results; therefore, if you have mainly text and narrative data, be sure to convert qualitative codes into quantitative counts, and always collect demographic information on the participants so that the quantitative requirement is covered. To meet this standard, you can even count how many times a participant received an intervention.

> *Did you know that you can convert qualitative data into quantitative data, but not quantitative into qualitative data? Simply count the frequency of codes and times a certain code is present to transition from qualitative to quantitative data.*

Frequencies, Percents, and Central Tendency: Descriptive Statistics

In SPSS, and as mentioned as the first thing to do when gearing up for your Results section, you will run statistics on frequencies and central tendencies. Central tendency is simply how the numbers tend to fall, and in the case of interval/ratio data, this is the mean, or average. For ordinal data, this measure is the median (the midpoint for all data), and for nominal data, the mode (the most answered item). Measures of variance (or dispersion) correspond to each central tendency measure, and these the author likes to call averages of difference, instead of averages of the same. Instead of how the numbers are alike, dispersion looks at how they are different. Table 6.4 shows each corresponding central tendency measure with its variance measure.

TABLE 6.4 CENTRAL TENDENCY AND VARIANCE

Level of measurement	Central tendency	Variance
Interval/ratio	Mean	Standard deviation
Ordinal	Median	Range
Nominal	Mode	Minimum-maximum

The two actions required for descriptive statistics analyses in SPSS are (1) selecting the appropriate commands for statistical analysis that are dependent on your data and their levels of measurement, and (2) selecting the interesting findings for reporting in the Results section. With SPSS running in front of you (you can do these commands from both the data and variables views; the tabs do not change), run the descriptive statistics:

1. Under the *Analyze* tab, select *Descriptive Statistics* and then select *Frequencies*.
2. Highlight all variables of interest and use the arrow between the columns to move these variables over to the right.
3. Select *Statistics* at the bottom; check *Mean, Median, Mode* at the right; check *Std. Deviation, Range, Minimum, Maximum* at the bottom left; and then *Continue* (right).
4. This takes you back to the original dialog box; select *Charts* at the bottom.
5. Select *Bar Charts, Pie Charts*, OR *Histograms*, depending on the level of measurement (use bar and pie for nominal/ordinal and select *percentages*; use histogram for interval/ratio) and then select *Continue* (right).
6. Back at the original dialog box, select *OK*.

What you will get looks something like these two SPSS outputs, the first being the statistics table (figure 6.1).

		Age	Gender	Posttest
N	Valid	35	33	30
	Missing	0	2	5
Mean		25	1	4
Median		23.5	1.5	3.5
Mode		25	1	4
Std. deviation		26.5	2	5.5
Range		5	2	4
Minimum		24	1	1
Maximum		28	2	4

FIGURE 6.1 SPSS OUTPUT: Descriptive Statistics

For each variable, there is a frequency table (see figure 6.2). In this figure, *valid* is the number of participants answering the item; *missing* is the number who did not. You will get a statistic for all requests, and it is up to you to match the numbers with their relevant level of measurement for the variable. For example, if *age* is measured by a real number, interval/ratio, then report the mean and standard deviation. If *gender* is measured by a nominal variable, with 1 = female and 2 = male, report the mode and minimum/maximum. If *posttest* is measured by a Likert ordinal ranking scale, with 4 being *strongly agree*, then report the median or mode, and range or minimum/maximum. In the frequency tables, you will have three percents reported: *percent* is the percent including missing cases, *valid* is the percent without missing cases added (use this one in your charts), and *cumulative* is the sum of percents from the beginning level of a variable up to the last one. *Frequency* in this table is the count or number of people answering at a certain level of the variable, such as female. These numbers can be put into a sentence: "There were 35 participants (*n* = 35) in the sample, the majority being women (55%) and the remainder men (45%)."

Age		Frequency	Percent	Valid percent	Cumulative percent
Valid	28	3	9	9	9
	27	4	11	11	20
	26	3	9	9	29
	25	22	62	62	91
	24	3	9	9	100
Total		35	100	100	

Gender	Frequency	Percent	Valid percent	Cumulative percent
Valid				
Male	15	43	45	45
Female	18	51	55	100
Missing	2	6		
Total	35	100	100	

Posttest		Frequency	Percent	Valid percent	Cumulative percent
Valid	1	1	3	3	3
	2	5	14	17	20
	3	4	12	13	33
	4	20	57	67	100
Missing		5	14		
Total		35	100	100	

FIGURE 6.2 SPSS OUTPUT: Descriptive Statistics Frequency Table

Figure 6.3 shows these percentages and frequencies for demographic and posttest data. The average age of participants was 25 (*M* = 25, *SD* = 26.5) years old (*n* = 22, 62%). Of these participants, most replied that they strongly agreed that services were satisfactory (*n* = 20, 67%). To place these results into a chart, match the numbers above in the SPSS output into the correct categories for which you have created fields and cells, and use the numbers above as a model for figure 6.3.

	M	*SD*	Mode	Range
Age	25	26.5		
Gender			4	4
Strongly agree that services were satisfactory			1	2

FIGURE 6.3 DESCRIPTIVE STATISTICS FREQUENCY TABLE

Correlations

Correlations are simply the association, or relationship, between two variables: bivariate correlations. They are either related or not, and can be related in a positive direction or a negative, or inverse, direction. There are two correlations you can run, either a Pearson (for two interval/ratio variables) correlation, or a Spearman (for two nominal/ordinal variables). If you have an interval/ratio variable you want to compare with a nominal/ordinal variable, use the Spearman correlation. If there is a negative sign before the correlation coefficient, then this is a negative relationship, meaning one variable increases while the other decreases. The thing to note is that these correlation tests—bivariate analysis in SPSS—do not tell you which one is going up and which one is going down in a negative relationship. (An alternative is to run partial correlations that will give a better idea of what goes up and what goes down.) If such is the case with nominal/ordinal variables, run a chi-square test to see the proportions of the variables across their response levels. For example, gender is negatively related to grade. Using a chi-square, if these variables are measured in nominal/ordinal levels, then you can discover which levels (male or female) are larger percentages in certain grades. Your intention when running correlations is to show what characteristics are related to others, which can say interesting things about your sample, as well as suggest items that need further study and may help you in suggesting service delivery improvements to your agency of study.

Here are the steps for running bivariate correlations:

1. Under the *Analyze* tab, select *Correlate* and then select *Bivariate*.
2. Highlight all variables of interest and use the arrow between the columns to move these variables over to the right.
3. Select Pearson at the bottom if these are interval/ratio variables; if not, select *Spearman*. SPSS will default to *two-tailed* for significance and *flag significant correlations*. Ensure that these options are selected.
4. Select *OK*.

The SPSS output looks similar to figure 6.4. *Correlation* reports the coefficient statistic, *significance* reports if error is less than .05 or .01, and *df* is degrees of freedom (the more the merrier). Note that the table can be folded diagonally and the numbers transpose (are the same on either side of the diagonal). A coefficient that equals 1 means that the variable is a perfect match; it is the exact same variable. A coefficient of -1 is the perfect opposite. Comparing *age* to itself shows a coefficient of 1; it is the same thing because it is comparing itself to itself. Age related to posttest is significant because the *significance* statistic is less than .05. (The Spearman should be run, not the Pearson, because there are nominal/ordinal levels of measurement.) The correlation coefficient is .494. *Gender* and *posttest* are negatively related to each other, but are not significant. There are six correlations in this table, a 3 x 3, with three variables compared to each other, two at a time, in a bivariate analysis. Taking these numbers and putting them into a sentence yields: "Three correlations were computed among age, gender, and posttest variables."

		Age	Gender	Posttest
Age	Correlation	1.00	.252	.494*
	Significance (2-tailed)		.102	.04
	df	0	28	28
Gender	Correlation	.252	1.00	−.301
	Significance (two-tailed)	.102		.07
	df	28	0	28
Posttest	Correlation	.494*	−.301	1.00
	Significance (two-tailed)	.04	.07	
	df	28	28	0

*Significant at $p < .05$.

FIGURE 6.4 SPSS OUTPUT: Correlations

Figure 6.5 shows bivariate correlation results. One of the six correlations was statistically significant and was equal to .494 for a positive association between age and posttest scores. Although not statistically significant, one coefficient, gender and posttest, was negative, showing an inverse relationship among these two variables. To place these results into a chart, match the numbers above in the SPSS output into the correct categories for which you have created fields and cells, and use the numbers above as a model for figure 6.5.

	Age	Gender
Gender	.252	
Posttest	.494*	−.301

FIGURE 6.5 CORRELATIONS TABLE

Chi-Square

A chi-square (χ^2) test simply looks at what you would expect to see as opposed to what the numbers show. It is used with nominal/ordinal levels of measurement, but if you have many levels or ranks for an ordinal variable, it can get a bit confusing because the percentages/proportions are dispersed across these many levels and you will find that you have small differences in percentages because they are spread thin across said levels. Chi-square conceptually is telling you that, if everything were equal across your numbers, then you would expect the percentages of your samples to fall evenly across the item responses (e.g., half should be male and half female). Then it compares this expectation against what you do have in your item responses (the *observed*), and it tells you that, if this is so different from the expected, there is a statistically significant association between those levels of how participants answered. For example, there are more females who answered that they were satisfied with the intervention than males. These statistics are given in percentages, which when the decimal is moved two places left becomes a proportion, the portion of a whole. You would express this association that is unexpected and observed in your numbers as the variable female being associated positively with being satisfied.

Following is a step-by-step procedure for running a chi-square:

1. Under the *Analyze* tab, select *Descriptive Statistics* and then select *Crosstabs*.
2. Highlight one variable of interest and use the arrow between the columns to move this variable over to the right to the *Row* field.
3. Highlight the next variable of interest and use the arrow between the columns to move this variable over to the right to the *Column* field.
4. Select *Statistics* at the bottom; check *Chi-square* and then *Continue* (right).
5. This takes you back to the original dialog box; select *Cells* (bottom).
6. Select *Observed, Expected,* and under *Percentages,* check *Row, Column, Total* and then select *Continue* (right).
7. Back at the original dialog box, select *OK*.

The SPSS output is shown in figure 6.6. Although you see in the chi-square test that the crosstab model is not statistically significant because the Pearson chi-square is greater than .05 (.102 > .05), the contingency table is interesting and worth describing in your Results. What is interesting is that, when you look at the larger percentages of counts in the table, you will see that the highest percentage is *strongly agree* and *female* (at 44%).

You will also see that, for males, larger percentages lie in *strongly disagree* and *disagree*. It is reasonable to say that females felt more satisfied by the intervention than males, and that this observation requires further investigation. This test result can be expressed in sentence format as follows: "A one-sample chi-square was conducted for associations between gender and posttest scores of intervention satisfaction. The results of the test were not statistically significant, χ^2 (4, N = 33) = 7.435, p = .102. Although not statistically significant, the contingency table shows interesting associations between gender and intervention satisfaction. The proportion of males was greater than that of females when strongly disagreeing that the intervention was satisfactory (P = .33). An even greater proportion than dissatisfaction was females strongly agreeing that the intervention was satisfactory (P = .44)."

	Posttest				
	Strongly disagree	***Disagree***	***Agree***	***Strongly agree***	**Total**
Gender					
Male					
Count	5	5	3	2	15
Expected count	3.75	3.75	3.75	3.75	15.0
% within gender	33%	33%	20%	13%	100.0%
Female					
Count	2	3	5	8	18
Expected count	4.5	4.5	4.5	4.5	18.0
% within gender	11%	17%	28%	44%	100.0%
Total					
Count	7	8	8	10	33
Expected count	8.25	8.25	8.25	8.25	33.0%
% within gender	21.2%	24.2%	24.2%	30.3%	100.0%

FIGURE 6.6 SPSS OUTPUT: Chi-Square

Figure 6.7 shows these differences between gender and post-test answers.

	Posttest scores of intervention satisfaction	
	Strongly disagree observed proportions	*Strongly agree* observed proportions
Male	.33	.13
Female	.11	.44

FIGURE 6.7 CHI-SQUARE TABLE

t-Tests

A *t*-test is simply a comparison of means, and although that sounds simple, it is not so simple to read. If you get lucky enough to run a *t*-test with variables that have interval/ratio levels of measurement, you must take into account effect size, and this is truly a follow-up test: Cohen's *d*. Effect size measures whether the changes from pretest to posttest are large enough to attribute said changes to the intervention; it should always be run and reported when analyzing *t*-tests in program evaluation and is the perfect program evaluation statistic. The power worksheet (worksheet 6.2) will describe this in more detail.

A *t*-test is novel for the program evaluation Results section; however, the author suggests only conducting a *t*-test with two interval/ratio variables; it makes more sense and the math is not so fuzzy. If you do run a *t*-test, you can show the difference between pretest and posttest scores, which in the end is what you really want to do in a program evaluation: to show that clients improved from before the intervention to after the intervention because of the intervention. If you want to become a *t*-test evaluator, you should have some say in the design and data collection for the measurement, pretest and posttest, and become a master at this statistic. You can conduct an independent samples *t*-test with an interval/ratio variable compared to a nominal variable, and you delineate the dichotomous nominal variable in the syntax for specified values as 1 and 2 in the group cells.

A paired samples *t*-test requires only three steps:

1. Under the *Analyze* tab, select *Compare Means* and then select *Paired Samples*.
2. Highlight the two variables of interest (they must be an interval/ratio level of measurement) and use the arrow between the columns to move them to the right.
3. Select *OK*.

Figure 6.8 shows SPSS output for a *t*-test with an interval/ratio variable (age) and an ordinal variable (posttest) that we are treating as interval/ratio as an example only. It is important to note that some of the output provided is created rather than exact for ease of understanding.

		Mean	N	Std. deviation	Std. error mean
Pair 1	Age	25	22	26.5	23.3
	Posttest	4	20	3.3	2.3

a. Paired Samples Statistics

		N	Correlation	Sig.
Pair 1	Age Posttest	20	.454	.013

b. Paired Samples Correlations

Paired differences

	Mean	Std. deviation	Std. error mean	95% confidence interval		*t*-test	*df*	Sig. (two-tailed)
Pair 1				Lower	Upper			
Age Posttest	10.2	12.2	5.4	8.5	13.2	11.45	19	.04

c. Paired Samples Test

FIGURE 6.8 SPSS OUTPUT: Paired Samples *t*-Tests

These statistics can be expressed in sentence format: "A paired samples *t*-test was run to investigate if age was more of a factor than posttest scores. The mean for age (*M* = 25, *SD* = 26.5) was significantly greater than the posttest mean (*M* = 4, *SD* = 3.3), *t* (20) = 11.45, *p* < .05." All we are saying here is that the average age is greater than the hypothetical (if posttest were a true number) average of a posttest score. If posttest were measured as a dichotomous variable, such as 1 = yes, 2 = no for satisfaction with the intervention, an independent samples *t*-test would be appropriate. Worksheet 6.2 provides information on how to analyze effect size that goes hand in hand with *t*-tests to show whether there was enough of a change from pretest to posttest scores to truly say that the change was due to the intervention. The power descriptions below also explain differences in the *power* concept.

Worksheet 6.2

STATISTICAL POWER (GRAVETTER AND WALLNAU, 2009)

1. Power simply means the probability that the test will correctly reject a false null hypothesis, meaning that the stats will indicate that there really is an effect when there really is an effect. It is the size or magnitude of the treatment effect. Researchers usually calculate power beforehand to determine if a treatment is likely to be successful. Sample size, size of treatment effect, one- or two-tailed tests, and alpha level affect power.
2. You can use power to determine the strength of a treatment effect as an alternative to measuring effect size directly. Power and effect size are related.
3. Effect size is a component of power, but power is the umbrella for other components, such as the following:
   a. Directional hypothesis: You have a directional hypothesis (one tail) that the critical region is on

one side of the distribution. There are no calculations here; you defend why you chose directional. One-tailed tests increase the power.

b. Alpha level: If it is too small, you may miss an effect, Type II error, but .001, .01, and .05 are most common in behavioral stats. There are no calculations here; you defend your selection of the alpha level. Reducing the alpha reduces the power.

c. Sample size: The bigger the better (the law of large numbers and the central limit theorem), and the bigger you get, the closer you are to the true population. The bigger the sample, the better the power. The calculation here is standard error (SE) for sample mean.

d. Treatment effect: For calculations for the treatment effect, such as eta squared (the variance explained), or Cohen's *d* for *t*-tests, the more you can explain, the better.

So . . . you have nothing to do but defend your alpha, directional hypothesis, and sample size (SE is already listed in SPSS results). For the effect size part, this is eta squared and you can explain this in text and table if you wish.

PICTURES, TABLES, AND CHARTS:
FUN STUFF LIKE SMART ART

The Results section is challenging because it presents the numbers and/or text (for qualitative findings). Also, organizing information is necessary, but this process can at first appear complicated and complex. Consider how it is easiest for you to understand numbers, such as those in your checkbook, which is organized through a ledger. You are doing something similar—placing those numbers into an organized format. The best way to do this is through a table, chart, or graph. This is especially important when you are trying to create a readable Results sections; many people simply look at the tables and do not read the sentences describing the numerical findings. In the writing, it is imperative to use those fancy terms and words and then to express them in visual form, such as a simpler table and/or graph. Although this is a technical section, you can make it understandable and credible. Again, you know the numbers and findings better than anyone else. It is now time to present the interesting items you found when you ran the statistics and themes in the qualitative data.

> *When you write the Results section, have beside you an APA cheat sheet, your favorite basic research methods book, and a program evaluation article. These tools will help with referencing technical terms, in-text citations, and Results section formatting.*

Microsoft Word can be extremely helpful in presenting your findings. You can insert a table or chart and add Smart Art to show processes or models. Spend some time playing around with these functions to best present findings in graphic form. When you use tables and charts, be sure to title them, explain what they represent, and number them (e.g., table 1). These steps can enhance your readers' ability to understand, in the simplest form, just what it is you are trying to convey in your findings. They are like adding pictures to a book, affording the visual learner more opportunity to grasp your outcomes.

Demographics

Consider the demographics section as your way of showing just who the participants/consumers/recipients of the intervention are—a profile so to speak. Most percentages will be in the demographics section. You are simply reporting the percentages, means, and modes, for example, in tabular form. Select the variables that are most interesting to you and to the agency, which may be all your variables, and organize them into a table.

Correlations

Remember that the SPSS output of correlations is duplicated along the middle diagonal so be sure to present these statistics only once. Again, select the most interesting, which may or may not be statistically significant, and place them into a table. In the author's experience, students find negative correlations that are of interest, and this is the best place to present them as items for further study within the delivery of an intervention.

Additional Statistics

After demographics and correlations, you want to add follow-up tests, such as chi-square and *t*-tests, to the interesting findings. With chi-square, select the levels of a variable that follow up correlations of interest, such as negative ones or statistically significant ones, and present the percentages for each level of the two variables in a table. With *t*-tests, present the means of variables in a table. There will be less to select from with *t*-tests because you will probably have fewer, or just one, test; hence, you should present these in full. Remember to keep it simple while showing the technical parts of statistics, such as coefficients, and think of how you would best understand the findings in a table or chart.

PRESENTING QUALITATIVE FINDINGS

It is suggested that qualitative findings should be placed after the quantitative ones. Use subheadings to represent the themes found; then describe them in the narrative. Unlike statistical reporting, which uses the APA sentence structure, qualitative reporting has no uniform formatting. Do keep these findings neutral, factual, and direct. Present the type of code found (a first- or second-level code) and use the quotes as your evidence to back up the theme. Do the same for all themes you wish to present that are pertinent to your findings. Be sure to have both introductory and concluding paragraphs for the coding themes; within these paragraphs, assert your major findings from the qualitative data. Be as parsimonious as possible (keep it short and sweet) because text requires more space than numbers; these results can become very lengthy if you are not careful. Use tables to list larger themes (see figure 6.9); add brief descriptions below the themes; and add graphics to represent action, flow, or process between themes.

Resistance	Need assertion	Benefit
Uncertainty about services	Vocalizes need in intervention	Notices changes due to intervention
Past service discrepancies	Requests made from intervention staff	Applies intervention skill to increase quality of life

FIGURE 6.9 QUALITATIVE THEMES TABLE EXAMPLE

Qualitative Tables and Graphics

Qualitative codes can lend themselves to interesting graphics and tables, through the use of what might be called an *archetype* or typical client. You can place these codes in a table, along with brief descriptions, or you can name certain groupings of characteristics and present the labels with the codes found for each. For example, you may find that clients satisfied with the intervention are also verbal and expressive and that they completed the intervention. You can present these characteristics of the satisfied client in a table. Also, when you want to show a process or action that is found in the themes and patterns, you can present qualitative codes in Smart Art. There may be stages or levels found in the data, such as doing one action before another, and Smart Art can be used to reveal these processes. For example, you may find in qualitative data that a satisfied client is first resistant to services, then asserts her needs, and then benefits from the intervention. You will then want to show the process of becoming a satisfied client (see figure 6.10).

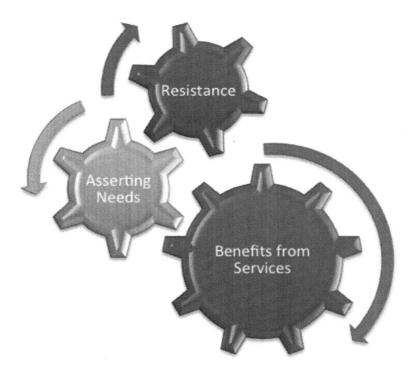

FIGURE 6.10 QUALITATIVE THEMES GRAPHIC EXAMPLE

THE PROCESS OF WRITING RESULTS

If you find yourself getting confused and overwhelmed when you look at your stats and then try to present them in charts and write about them, I suggest compartmentalizing them—after you take a break. Take one section at a time; for example, look at the Demographics section first and then move on to Correlations. Concern yourself only with showing who the participants are; complete that piece and then move on. Keep in mind your purpose, such as showing the reader who participated in the intervention, and express this in a simple yet technical way by throwing in those research terms. Also remember that you know these numbers best, and although the process may feel foreign to you, you can do this. Maybe, just maybe, you will find yourself intrigued with the challenge of helping others to understand what you have found and just how interesting it truly is!

Worksheet 6.3 will help you put all these steps together into a readable Results section. Remember to take a break when your head starts to hurt, and be sure that you have saved the database, including the output, in a couple of places. Use writing guides such as an APA cheat sheet and other program evaluation articles, and include the technical research jargon. You do not need to define technical terms, but use them as descriptors and always back up any assertions you make with statistical findings by including the statistical coefficients and percentages in the sentence.

Worksheet 6.3

HOW TO DO THE RESULTS SECTION

Decide on the heading/title for the Results section, Results or Findings (pick one and use it uniformly). Either is fine, and you will see both Findings and Results in empirical papers. Subheadings will be listed below.

Discuss what you found in your quantitative and/or qualitative data analysis; mention the types of methods you used in your data analysis (quantitative statistical analysis on SPSS of regression, chi square, etc., and/or first- and second-level qualitative coding using multiple coders for trustworthiness). Remember that in journal articles this section usually talks about the statistics (in quantitative methods) and/or includes text about the coding and patterns (in qualitative methods).

You must include in the Results section the statistical tests you used and/or the qualitative coding you completed. You may use other articles and the statistics help sheet as a guide for doing so.

1. Demographics: Immediately tell your reader about the group that received the intervention and their characteristics. Did they all complete the intervention, what made them eligible for the intervention, and were they all in the same group or were there other groups receiving other interventions (comparison groups)?

   In paragraph form, provide a descriptive profile of the persons who participated in the intervention:

   _____

   _____

   _____

2. Comparison of pretest and the posttest scores: Talk about the findings from the scores at the beginning of the intervention and how they compare to the scores taken after the intervention was delivered. What do they show and what is or is not significant?

Pretest scores: _____

Intervention delivery: _____

Posttest scores: _____

3. Analysis: Describe the tests you used to analyze the data and what you found. For quantitative analysis, did you use descriptive and/or inferential statistics and/or did you use regression or ANOVA? Why did you select the tests that you used, and what did you find? What was significant and what was not? For qualitative analysis, what was the process for analyzing interviews and what patterns and themes did you find? What are some quotes to support your findings?

    Quantitative analysis: State the statistical analysis you conducted and what variables were or were not significant (for example, regression revealed that the intervention worked better for females than males).

    Qualitative analysis: Describe the themes and codes and give hypothetical quotes from your data analysis. (For example, coding revealed that concern about finances played a large part in intervention participation, seen in the following quote . . . .)

4. Table, chart, and/or graph: Draft a table, chart, and/or graph with data to show what your sample looks like (see figure 6.11). Use other graphs for guidance. It is suggested that you simply show in averages and frequencies your demographic profile for the cases in your study evaluation. In the graph, make columns for how many participated (n = ?) and the percentage of cases that were male/female or of a specific ethnicity, age, education level, or class/income, for example. Also

make a graph of what variables were significant, showing that your intervention worked for certain groups
(specify these groups) in the program evaluation.

Example table	Ethnicity	Education	Age	Completed program
Male	n = ?/%	n = ?/%	n = ?/%	n = ?/%
Female	n = ?/%	n = ?/%	n = ?/%	n = ?/%

Example table	N = ?	Pretest scores	Posttest scores	Significance
Male				
Female				

FIGURE 6.11 RESULTS SECTION TABLE EXAMPLES

5. Extra Points: You can gain extra points by discussing
   validity with regard to external threats and controls
   (can you generalize your findings to other groups?) and
   internal threats and controls (did something else cause
   the change?), outcomes (were your outcomes what you
   anticipated?), and standards of evaluation (how did you
   maintain utility, feasibility, propriety, and accuracy in
   your data analysis?).
   Controls for external and internal validity: _____
   Anticipated outcomes: _____
   Evaluation standards: _____

RESULTS TERMS

Correlation (co-relate): Variables that show an association or relationship, either positive or negative, to each other.

Bivariate (bivariable): Two variables in an analysis, such as one variable compared to another.

Univariate (uni-variable): One variable in an analysis, such as a percentage of one variable.

Multivariate: Many variables in an analysis, compared to each other in groups and outside of group differences.

Degrees of freedom: From a sample size, the amount of "left-over" cases after statistical tests are conducted. The larger the sample, the smaller the possible error and the larger the degrees of freedom; it's a good thing.

Statistic: A number that is the final result of a mathematical equation or formula, such as a coefficient or *t*-test; a single number representing the final outcome of an equation.

Significance: The probability that a statistical test conducted on a sample is not due to chance.

Effect size: A change between a pretest and a posttest that is big enough to show an impact from the treatment.

7 Discussion

IT'S ALMOST OVER. YOU WILL soon successfully complete an evaluation study! (Be sure to add this in bold to your résumé.) You may also find that, in addition to feeling excited that this process will soon be over, you are feeling exhausted by the arduous learning process. Because this is a common occurrence, I suggest that, as you walk through this research study, you take notes from the beginning that will be unique to the Discussion section. As you conduct this project, you will have thoughts about what should be studied next, the more interesting findings of your project, and how you might enhance an intervention and its outcome measurement. Now is the time to write about these thoughts.

The Discussion section breaks down the technical, numerical, and possibly lengthy Results section and transforms it into readable and layperson-oriented issues that can be used in future research. By summarizing your study in the Discussion, you share with the readers and stakeholders of your evaluation what is most important in the outcomes and the suggestions that originated from the Results. When you write the Discussion, make notes of what you want it to be without looking at your results. Write down your thoughts, questions, and concerns about the entire study. This is the time to share your experience and knowledge about the evaluation in a format that is honest, projective, and helpful to the agency and to the persons who benefit from the intervention.

There are requirements for including your thoughts and ideas in the Discussion section, with the purpose of summarizing the study and providing tidbits for the agency to use for future study, evaluation, grant writing, and funding: (1) summarizing in a manner that stakeholders can apply, (2) presenting the limitations of your research, (3) offering suggestions in an empowering way for improvement and facilitation of future study, and (4) providing implications for this future evaluation research. Keep in mind that, within these requirements, there are two primary standards: increased quality of life for participants and help and empowerment for the agency delivering the intervention. Keeping these standards at the forefront will help you write the content and increase the utility and impact of your Discussion section.

THE AFTERMATH OF DATA ANALYSIS AND PRESENTING RESULTS: MAKING LEMONADE

Depending on the agency and its data, as well as your intimacy with these data, you may be facing the challenge of how to communicate the importance of a minimal amount of data or data that do not necessarily show program efficacy. This is the problem of how to make lemonade when your study gives you lemons. You have managed to place these limited findings into a narrative and tabular format in the Results section; now you must impart its importance. This is a good place to include possible pretests and posttests and survey and measurement prospects and to make your suggestions. You can also applaud the agency for using what it has and for collecting data for outcomes in the first place. This is really all about how you spin your message. It is easier to understand and convince others of the importance of your evaluation research when you are positive, as opposed to blaming and finger-pointing. Spin your message in a positive way and you will convince others of the significance of this research, as well as the value of your intervention and evaluation assistance to the agency in terms of possible continued or even increased funding in the future. Even if there is a minimal amount of data collected, and the program does not appear efficacious based on your findings, you can point out that there were data and that efforts are being made to evaluate the intervention. With some adjustments to outcome measurement and possibly even delivery of the intervention, the process can be exponentially improved. Consider in your writing: if participants did not have access to the intervention, would they have had any assistance at all? This can lead to the argument for continued and improved measurement for outcomes, as well as the necessity of the agency's intervention.

In the Discussion you will be presenting suggestions for improvement. Conventionally these suggestions would include continued and furthered research to add to the knowledge base, improvement in outcome measurement, increased and/or continued funding for the social service provided, and issues related to the improvement of the quality of life for the participants. Such improvements need to originate from the strengths of the intervention evidenced by your evaluation study and used to formulate action-based research suggestions.

ACTION-BASED RESEARCH

Action-based research and/or participatory action research can steer your Discussion section onto an exciting and empowering path. Stringer (1999) presents a model of action-based research that transposes onto evaluation research; the primary components are experience, data gathering, analysis, representation, and action. Although it is most beneficial to begin with an action-based evaluation method—one that is driven by recipients of the intervention—you may not have this luxury. Because you are not determining the design a priori and you are interacting only with agency stakeholders and intervention deliverers, you are conducting secondary research. However, in a sense, you are conducting action-based research because, from the perspective of the agency as client in evaluation research, you approached the agency first and requested that it dictate the purpose of your study: what would be beneficial to the agency and what could provide it with edification in the future, especially in terms of outcomes that would support grant writing and future funding. If the outcomes are less than stupendous, or even marginal, you might provide only the data analysis, allowing the agency contact to decipher the results and also to provide ideas for measurement improvement to ensure that all research analysis bases are covered. The action-based research component is delivery, in objective fashion, of the results only; the agency must decide what to do with these results.

As opposed to traditional evaluation research, action-based research offers understanding of client-directed experience and a place to celebrate the findings with participant representation and action. We have established that the initial contact and directive for the evaluation came from the agency; what is the best way to celebrate and apply the findings with that agency? A creative and useful product is suggested and described in the section "Creatively Presenting Your Product." Additional tactics include sharing your findings directly with the agency personnel with whom you have been working, taking photographs with them and participants, having a party to celebrate the conclusion of the study, and having brainstorming sessions with agency personnel and participants about what they want to next discover and examine about their intervention. A strategic plan can be devised, including suggestions and integrating data management and data collection processes. It can really be fun, and empowering, to share your knowledge and process with the recipients of your evaluation research. These action-based research elements can be written into the Discussion section.

IMPLICATIONS: POLICY, RESEARCH, PRACTICE, AND THEORY

The Discussion needs to include implications for all areas of social work. These implications address edification of our discipline, as well as affirmation of the important evaluation research that was conducted. All intervention evaluations can address the primary elements of social work in policy, research, practice, and finally theory. Theory is important to social work because it adds to the knowledge base as well as formulating unique processes for social service delivery. The qualitative findings can be most helpful in deriving theory implications, and you can suggest ideas for future theory development from themes and patterns. You can even develop client-based theory in more radical qualitative methodologies, such as classic grounded theory.

Some examples of policy implications are client- and agency-driven measures of advocacy, such as effectual policy (e.g., funding to increase the quality of life for marginalized populations). For research, there always needs to be more research, especially research that integrates client- and agency-based evaluation directives. In addition to this research implication, mentioning the publication of your project is essential to building the knowledge base of social work evaluation research by providing models and replication opportunities to others with similar interventions for their own outcome assessment. Practice implications will depend on your description of the process of intervention delivery, including suggestions that may be relevant to resources, additional staff, outreach, and client needs as well as empowerment. Finally, social work theory is often neglected in evaluation research; the qualitative findings and emergent theory in your research can offer opportunities to address this problem.

Do think of organizing the Discussion section and summary of your evaluation to emphasize two key elements: (1) the major outcomes of the intervention and (2) support for the evaluation research completed and suggested by this study. Be sure to summarize and describe the most important findings of the research while suggesting ways to facilitate data management and future outcome measurement so that others can understand and apply your findings for the edification of both the recipients and the deliverers of this intervention. You want to leave your reader intrigued and invested in both the research and the client. Worksheet 7.1 will walk you through the items addressed and described above.

Worksheet 7.1

HOW TO DO THE DISCUSSION SECTION

Your Discussion/Conclusion section explains in plain language what the Results section explained in statistical and technical jargon; you break the technical content down for readers so that they take away the highlights from your evaluation study. You may also base this section on your current knowledge, which has increased as you progressed through your design and evaluation of an existing intervention. Perhaps you may have noted in your literature review that there was little published on the intervention, that the intervention has been adapted many times so that it difficult to find common themes, or that the research studies in your literature review had poor sampling or biased techniques, for example. This is where you mention what you have learned overall. Be practical in your discussion and base your recommendations on what you have learned thus far about the intervention, solidly rooted in your evaluation data and analyses. This is where you connect your research to social work practice, research-based practice, and best practices for specific populations. Ultimately, this is where you describe and explain that the program intervention evaluated is or is not efficacious and use this information to make recommendations.

Talk about what you will do with your evaluation (and don't forget to publish it!), how you will share it, what are the next steps, and what is needed for success. Address implications for social work theory, research, practice, and policy. Discuss how your outcomes contribute new, improved, and important information to the social work knowledge base.

The primary focus of this section is to highlight the most important, usually statistically significant or qualitatively salient, findings, repeated from the Results section in words and language that most readers can understand. Next, discuss the program evaluation in terms of practice and what the evaluation means for social service delivery. Speak of the evaluation in a practical, applied manner. What exactly does your program evaluation mean for social work? What should be done next or what exactly do the findings imply for the intervention? Next discuss the limitations of your study, for example, that it may/may not be based on self-reports and that you are an external evaluator who does not know the nuances of the intervention. Include any other items that make your evaluation less than perfect. Honesty is necessary. Finally, end the Discussion section with a paragraph that sums up your evaluation with a direction for future recommendations.

Select a heading/title, Discussion or Conclusion, and use it uniformly; either is fine and you will see both in empirical papers. Subheadings are listed below.

1. Highlighted findings (you will not see this subheading in a research article, but use it for the purposes of this paper): Highlight the overall significant findings of the program evaluation.

   _____

   _____

   _____

2. Practice Applications: Discuss the application of the evaluation to social work practice.

   _____

   _____

   _____

3. Implications: Discuss the evaluation in relation to its implications for social work practice, research, policy, and theory.
   Practice: _____
   Research: _____
   Policy: _____
   Theory: _____

4. Limitations: Mention the limitations of your study.
   Methodology: _____
   Sample: _____

5. Concluding paragraph: Summarize the main findings of your study with future recommendations.

   _____

   _____

   _____

CREATIVELY PRESENTING YOUR PRODUCT

Similar to the Discussion section, in which you provided content that is usable and understandable by the reader (especially important after the detail and technicality of the Methods and Results sections), a pamphlet or talking point document for the agency should present outcome messaging in layperson terms suitable for promotional use. This document should include an element of action-based research in which you provide a return to the participants, client, and/or agency as a thank you for letting you share in their experience. The author requires students to create such a document for the agency. Microsoft Publisher is the perfect software program for creating this product, which should contain major outcomes that promote the intervention/agency, as well as pictures, tables, and charts for easy and immediate understanding of both the population served and the evaluation findings. Talking points, pamphlets, and other similar products are invaluable to the agency, which may not currently have the means or opportunity to promote its outcomes.

Another idea for a creative project is one that is completely dictated by the student who completes the research study. This project has some relevance to the research conducted, but it is not presented in a traditional format such as a PowerPoint document, written paper, or even a pamphlet or talking points. Instead, the student must determine how to artistically present some element of the research in a nontraditional format, such as poetry, painting, photography, or even a diorama. Although it is challenging for some students to think outside the box when working with data, expressing their ideas and findings in artistic forms can be liberating. A project such as this can also make research more fun by providing an outlet to express findings in a truly personalized and creative way.

Figure 7.1 is a template that can be used for a creative product that reveals the results of the evaluation and promotes the social

5–10 sets of most pertinent outcomes, variables, correlations, and demographics

- Social service agency contact information
- Disclaimer about students conducting this research
- Blank if not needed for content

- Social service agency name
- Picture of agency, staff, and/or clients

a. Side One (dimensions may be 8 x 11 in. or determined by the student)

- Description and information about the social service intervention
- Agency mission and objectives

Outcomes tables, charts, and graphs

- Additional descriptions and information about the intervention
- Pictures

b. Side Two (dimensions are the same as for side one)

FIGURE 7.1 CREATIVE PROJECT TRIFOLD TEMPLATE

service; the knowledge gained from the evaluation and the content that the agency wishes to promote will determine what is included in this product. Include as much visual material as possible, such as pictures and tables, and less textual content; the goal is to catch the reader's eye.

PUTTING IT ALL TOGETHER

Upon completion of the Discussion section, you will need to synchronize the worksheets provided in this manual. This process is summarized below in worksheet 7.2. When you combine all the elements of your project, remember the universal research recipe: literature, methods, results, and discussion.

Worksheet 7.2

OVERVIEW FOR THE FINAL EVALUATION PAPER

Remember that this is a technical research manuscript. Use subheadings and titles, not numbers. The numbering below is for outlining purposes only. Refer to the worksheets and rubrics in the manual for required elements within each section. You can reclaim missed points in the Literature Review and Methods sections by integrating these edits into the final paper. Note that the Practice Evaluation goes in the Appendices, not in the body of the paper.

1. Title Page (using specific words that name the intervention evaluated)
2. Table of Contents (optional; if you're feeling fancy)
3. Abstract (or Executive Summary)
4. Literature Review
5. Methods
6. Results (including charts and tables that display statistics and qualitative codes)
7. Discussion
8. References
9. Appendices:
   a. Logic model (referred to in Literature Review)
   b. Measurement in use by the program (referred to in Methods)
   c. Data entry logs (referred to in Methods)
   d. Excel database screen shot (referred to in Methods)
   e. SPSS database screen shot (referred to in Methods)
   f. New and improved measurement (referred to in Methods)

g. Outcome pamphlet and/or talking points to be given to the agency or your professor (referred to in Results)
h. The new and improved measurement in the Discussion as an enhancement for the agency (optional)
i. Any creative project that is directly related to your research evaluation
j. Any other items that you wish to use to reveal your research brilliance and fabulous program evaluation!

The new parts need to be added after the final paper is completed:

1. Abstract: The abstract should consist of four to five sentences in this order:
   a. Purpose and need for the study
   b. Methods, design, sample, and the intervention
   c. Findings or results
   d. Conclusions and recommendations for social work
   The abstract should be followed by your revised literature review, methods, results, and discussion, with the practice evaluation included in an appendix.
2. References
3. Appendices
   a. Your logic model
   b. Budget
   c. Your data collection instrument
   d. Practice evaluation
   e. Any other extraneous but related information/materials (such as consent forms, confidentiality forms, and program materials)

A FINAL COMMENT

As the author, I sincerely hope that this simple hands-on evaluation research manual will be helpful to you in your social work research endeavors. When I began teaching research, I integrated all the technical elements of research into my courses, including randomization and experimental methods. I found that, as a PhD in social work, I understood these concepts, but I never used them, and wondered at their practicality. Hence, I am grateful to my students for their feedback. Over the years, my own reflection of how I conduct evaluation research opened me to the idea of teaching what is used most, in the most applicable way, and most simply. That really is the beauty of social work research: the process of adjusting to and being flexible about what we are working with, what we have, and what is the best way to convey these findings in a research context. If I could impart any wisdom to students and instructor alike, I would say that knowledge is accessible by all and that we, as social workers, can conduct the research easily. We can do the research especially well when we allow our clients and social service agencies to direct it toward what they want and need and toward what will effectively promote the vital social services they provide. Yes, research IS sexy!

References

Atkinson, R. (1998). *The life story interview*. Thousand Oaks, CA: Sage.

Bureau of Labor Statistics, U.S. Department of Labor (2012). Social workers. *2012–2013 Occupational Outlook Handbook*. Retrieved from http://www.bls.gov/ooh/community-and-social-service/social-workers.htm

Chapin, R. (1995). Social policy development: The strengths perspective. *Social Work, 40*(4), 506–514.

Chapin, R. (2011). *Social policy for effective practice: New directions in social work*. New York, NY: Routledge.

Clandinin, D. J. (2007). *Handbook of narrative inquiry*. Thousand Oaks, CA: Sage.

Council on Social Work Education. (2011). *2010 Statistics on social work education in the U.S.: A summary*. Alexandria, VA: Council on Social Work Education.

Cozby, P. C. (2007). *Methods in behavioral research* (9th ed.). Boston, MA: McGraw-Hill.

Craig, M., & Cook, L. (2007). *Doing ethnographies*. Thousand Oaks, CA: Sage.

Doran, G. T. (1981). There's a S.M.A.R.T. way to write management's goals and objectives. *Management Review, 70*(11), 35–36.

Epstein, I. (2001). Using available clinical information in practice-based research: Mining for silver while dreaming of gold. *Social Work in Health Care, 33*(3/4), 15–32.

153

Epstein, I., & Blumenfield, S. (2001). *Clinical data-mining in practice-based research: Social work in hospital settings.* Binghamton, NY: Haworth.

Faulkner, C., & Faulkner, S. (2014). *Research methods for social workers: A practice-based approach* (2nd ed.). Chicago, IL: Lyceum Books.

Fisher, R., & Karger, H. J. (1996). *Social work and community in a private world: Getting out in public* (1st ed.). Boston, MA: Allyn & Bacon.

Gibbons, J., & Gray, M. (2005). Teaching social work students about social policy. *Australian Social Work, 58*(1), 58–62.

Gravetter, F. J., & Wallnau, L. B. (2009). *Statistics for the behavioral sciences* (8th ed.). Belmont, CA: Wadsworth.

Greenwood, D. J., & Levin, M. (2007). *Introduction to action research: Social research for social change* (2nd ed.). Thousand Oaks, CA: Sage.

Grinnell, R. M., Gabor, P. A., & Unrau, Y. A. (2012). *Program evaluation for social workers: Foundations of evidence-based programs* (6th ed.). New York, NY: Oxford University Press.

Karger, H. J., & Stoesz, D. (2009). *American social welfare policy: A pluralist approach* (6th ed.). Boston, MA: Allyn & Bacon.

LaSala, M. C. (2003). When interviewing "family": Maximizing the insider advantage in the qualitative study of lesbians and gay men. In W. Meezan & J. L. Martin (Eds.), *Research methods with gay, lesbian, bisexual, and transgender populations* (pp. 15–30). New York, NY: Haworth Press.

Morgan, D. L. (1997). *Focus groups as qualitative research.* Thousand Oaks, CA: Sage.

Peake, K., & Epstein, I. (2004). Theoretical and practical imperatives for reflective social work organizations in health and mental health: The place of practice-based research. *Social Work in Mental Health, 3*(1/2), 23–37.

Stringer, E. T. (1999). *Action research* (2nd ed.). Thousand Oaks, CA: Sage.

Appendix

A

Research Resources

LITERATURE AND PROGRAM EVALUATION

American Evaluation Association, http://www.eval.org

Baumberger, M., Rugh, J., & Mabry, L. (2006). *Real world evaluation: Working under budget, time, data, and political constraints*. Thousand Oaks, CA: Sage.

Grinnell, R. M., Gabor, P. A., &. Unrau, Y. A. (2012). *Program evaluation for social workers: Foundations of evidence-based programs* (6th ed.). New York, NY: Oxford University Press.

Purdue University (2012). *Online Writing Lab (OWL)*. APA. Retrieved from https://owl.english.purdue.edu/

Unrau, Y. A., & Grinnell, R. M. (2005). The impact of social work research courses on research self-efficacy for social work students. *Social Work Education, 24*(6), 639–651.

METHODS

Faulkner, S. S., & Faulkner, C. A. (2013). *Research methods for social workers: A practice-based approach* (2nd ed.). Chicago, IL: Lyceum Books.

Grinnell, R. M. (2001). *Social work research and evaluation: Quantitative and qualitative approaches* (6th ed.). Itasca, IL: Peacock.

Grinnell, R. M., & Unrau, Y. A. (2008). *Social work research and evaluation: Foundations of evidence-based practice* (8th ed.). New York, NY: Oxford University Press.

RESULTS

Green, S. B., & Salkind, N. J. (2008). *Using SPSS for Windows and Macintosh: Analyzing and understanding data* (5th ed.). Upper Saddle River, NJ: Prentice Hall.

Nicol, A. A. M., & Pexman, P. M. (1999). *Presenting your findings: A practical guide for creating tables*. Washington, DC: American Psychological Association.

Phillips, J. L. (2001). *How to think about statistics* (6th ed.). New York: W. H. Freeman.

Salkind, N. J. (2004). *Statistics for people who (think they) hate statistics* (2nd ed.). Thousand Oaks, CA: Sage.

Tabachnick, B. G. (2001). *SPSS for Windows workbook to accompany Tabachnick and Fidell Using Multivariate Statistics* (4th ed.). Boston, MA: Allyn & Bacon.

Weinbach, R. W., & Grinnell, R. M. (2014) *Statistics for social workers* (9th ed.). Boston, MA: Allyn & Bacon.

QUALITATIVE METHODS

Belenky, M. F., Clinchy, B. M., Goldberger, N. R., & Tarule, J. M. (1986). *Women's ways of knowing*. New York, NY: BasicBooks.

Brearley, L. (2000). Exploring the creative voice in an academic context. *The Qualitative Report, 5*(3/4).

Collier, J. C., Jr., & Collier, M. (1986). *Visual anthropology: Photography as a research method*. Albuquerque, NM: University of New Mexico Press.

Creswell, J. W. (2006). *Qualitative inquiry and research design* (2nd ed.). Thousand Oaks, CA: Sage.

Denzin, N. K., & Lincoln, Y. S. (Ed.). (2005). *The Sage handbook of qualitative research* (3rd ed.). Thousand Oaks, CA: Sage.

Gilligan, C. (1982). *In a different voice.* Cambridge, MA: Harvard University Press.

Grinnell, R. M., & Unrau, Y. A. (2005). *Social work research and evaluation* (7th ed.). New York: Oxford University Press.

Guba, E. G. (1981).Criteria for assessing trustworthiness of naturalistic inquiries. *Educational Communication and Technology Journal, 29,* 75–91.

Kirk, J., & Miller, M. L. (1986). *Reliability and validity in qualitative research.* Thousand Oaks, CA: Sage.

Miller, J. B. (1986).*Toward a new psychology of women* (2nd ed.). Boston, MA: Beacon.

Neuman, W. L. (2006). *Social research methods.* Boston, MA: Pearson.

Ohnuki-Tierney, E. (1984). "Native" anthropologists. *American Anthropologist, 11,* 584–585.

Padgett, D. K. (1998). *Qualitative methods in social work research: Challenges and rewards.* Thousand Oaks, CA: Sage.

Pink, S. (2001). *Doing visual ethnography: Images, media and representation in research.* Thousand Oaks, CA: Sage.

Prosser, J. (Ed.). (1998). *Image-based research: A sourcebook for qualitative researchers.* Bristol, PA: Falmer Press.

Strauss, A., & Corbin, J. (1998). *Basics of qualitative research: Techniques and procedures for developing grounded theory* (2nd ed.). Thousand Oaks, CA: Sage.

B In-Class Exercises

CONDUCTING A FOCUS GROUP

Question: How Would You Improve This Class?

1. List questions and probes:

   _____

   _____

   _____

2. Ask the questions and take field notes:

   _____

   _____

   _____

3. Did you improvise with any questions? If so, what were the newly adapted questions?

   _____

   _____

   _____

4. What was the mood of the group?

_____

_____

_____

5. What visual observations did you make?

_____

_____

_____

6. What were themes in responses?

_____

_____

_____

7. What are your conclusions and recommendations?

_____

_____

_____

PRACTITIONER-RESEARCHER: PRACTICE-BASED RESEARCH EXERCISE IN FUNCTIONAL INQUIRY

■ The purpose of this case-scenario exercise is to place you in an event that may occur when you are in your future career.

■ You are taking the role of a practitioner-researcher to familiarize yourself with the process of conducting research in practice settings. This need to conduct research in practice and service delivery stems from your noticing a trend, change, or issue within your work environment. This will occur whether you are a direct practitioner or an administrative leader. In either role, the research process is the same (whether program or practice evaluation).

The flow of your questions and practice-based research process:

What's the biggest question?

What's the biggest need?

What do you want to know?

What are the extraneous issues that may or may not have an impact on your issue?

What is your method to collect information (data)?

Does the data need to be quantitative or qualitative or both?

Whom do you talk to (data sources)?

What resources are available to you?

Will anyone help you?

Where else will you collect data?

Statistical issues, service statistics, general statistics

Literature and recent studies on the topic of interest

What will you do with the information?

How will you reveal outcomes?

If needed, what changes will you advocate?

Feedback, how will you create a feedback loop and who will you include?

Now design your study and complete the methods:

1. Literature/Introduction/Need and Purpose:
2. Methodology:
3. Results:
4. Conclusions and Implications:

PRACTICE-BASED RESEARCH SCENARIOS

Administrative Leadership

Exercise 1
You are an auditor in a social service agency that is public and nonprofit and receives money and mandates from county, city, and state authorities. You do not have a caseload, but are in charge of auditing the records of all open cases (ranging from 400–500 cases at any time in the quarter) to ensure that funding mandates are followed and adhered to by staff that have direct contact with clients. You also are responsible for training all staff in the unit when needed.

You notice that there is a trend of staff turning in delayed and past-due required documentation.

Practice-based researcher, what do you do?

Exercise 2
You are the executive director of a small nonprofit agency that serves the homeless through case management, mainly by providing crisis linkage to more permanent services while providing no

physical services such as temporary housing or financial needs. Your agency provides an essential service, however, in assuring that homeless persons receive the services they require and is known as an agency that advocates for the homeless. You supervise one administrative staff and five case managers.

You notice that employee morale has changed, but you're not quite sure if this is positive or negative.

Practice-based researcher, what do you do?

Exercise 3

You are a mid-level manager in a large state-run agency that delivers social services to persons with HIV/AIDS. The unit you are responsible for has ten case managers and two administrative staff. Your unit is housed separately from the larger, central office and hospital for the social service. You answer to one person housed at the central office, an executive director. Your team has a recent addition, a new case manager, who has helped to decrease the already large caseloads.

You notice, after training, that the new-hire social worker has changed the dynamic of the office because she is assimilating well into the work culture. Some longer tenured workers are gossiping and feeling threatened by the new hire.

Practice-based researcher, what do you do?

Direct Practice

Exercise 4

You are a caseworker in Child Protective Services (CPS) and handle crisis calls, reports, and new intake cases and then assign them to caseworkers in the field to begin the allegation investigation. You are responsible for handling the first and initial call, providing crisis intervention if needed (call the police first?), and then assigning the case to an investigator with required follow-up in a month to determine the outcome of the case. You work in a team of five intake caseworkers, but you do not meet with persons face to face, only over the phone.

When you conduct your monthly follow-up, you notice in charting that there has been an increase in infant mortality.

Practice-based researcher, what do you do?

Exercise 5

You are a caseworker in a mid-size social service agency that serves adults who have special needs, such as seizure disorders and mental retardation. You are one of ten caseworkers in this office that provides intake, assessment, and casework covering placement and daily living needs. You are supervised by a mid-level manager and a unit supervisor. Administrative staff members assign incoming intakes to caseworkers on a rotating basis. All caseworkers carry a caseload of 75 persons, with or without intake, who are admitted to services.

You notice that you seem to be getting the majority of intakes that are admitted to the social service, thus increasing your caseload by 10 clients over the past week.

Practice-based researcher, what do you do?

Exercise 6

You work with severely mentally ill persons in an outpatient setting, providing long-term medication management services; treatment planning; and liaison with other service providers in a community, public, and state-run mental health clinic. You work with nurses, psychologists, psychiatrists, and other social workers like yourself in an interdisciplinary setting. You are responsible for monitoring your clients in the community by meeting with them at least once quarterly to ensure that they are stable and have no immediate issues or crises. Because the agency provides your clients with long-term services and clients will always be eligible for these services, you have very strong relationships with them.

You notice that many of your stable clients, 10 of them over the past two weeks, have suddenly become psychotic and require involuntary hospitalization in a state hospital.

Practice-based researcher, what do you do?

Administrative Leadership and Direct Practice

Exercise 7

You are a practitioner/supervisor who heads a small rural department of food stamp and WIC public services. You and your employees screen persons for eligibility, and if they are eligible based on the poverty level ($22,050 annual income for a family of four), your department ensures that they have this vital service delivered to them in the form of adequate food for families, whatever the agency's composition, as an effort to prevent hunger. You have worked in this agency for several years and have been promoted due to your diligent service, as both a direct practitioner and an administrative supervisor.

You notice that, after the federal government instigates fingerprinting as part of the eligibility screening process, there is a dramatic drop in returning clients and new intakes for services.

Practice-based researcher, what do you do?

DESIGN SCENARIO EXERCISES

Instructions

The instructions below apply to the five design scenario exercises that follow:

1. Decide what method is best (exploratory, explanatory, etc.).
2. Is this a quantitative and/or qualitative study, and why?

3. Draw the design notation (*X*, *O*, etc.).
4. Describe participants who will be included in the sample, such as the group receiving an intervention and their possible characteristics, and how you will secure the participation of these people.
5. What data collection instrument would you use?
6. What is your procedure for conducting the study?
7. List the independent variable(s). List the dependent variable(s).

Design Scenario 1

You're curious about why some persons with mental illness are incredibly creative, artful, and inventive. You're wondering about this because you work at an outpatient rehab clinic and have noticed this creativity in many of the clients, who are adults with mental illness. There is some but not a lot of literature on similar topics. There are some but not many theories on creativity and mental illness. How would you design this study?

Design Scenario 2

You work at a nonprofit social service agency that provides housing for the homeless. You have noticed in your dealings with clients that many of them are veterans with mental illness. There is a ton of research on this topic, but little explanation other than descriptive information, and absolutely no theories about what is occurring with this population. How would you design this study?

Design Scenario 3

You go to a conference and hear about a great new intervention that helps persons quickly and effectively resolve alcohol and drug abuse addictions; you are very impressed and want the agency where you work, a drug and alcohol counseling center, to implement this new and innovative intervention. The agency wants evidence, however, and the conference presenter gave very little evidence because the intervention is very new. How would you design a study to implement this intervention, in an evidence-based manner, at your work?

Design Scenario 4

You're an undergraduate research student who is assigned a study design to meet course requirements. Your life-long passion is your concern about the well-being of lab rats and what happens to them under research studies (in other departments, of course). You want to conduct a study to reveal the injustices against little white mice in research, and to invoke policy to protect them. How would you design this study to ensure that your political agenda is met?

Design Scenario 5

You are interested in the identity development of transgendered persons. However, there is little theory out there and you feel that transgendered persons have not been heard nor had their issues presented in the literature you have reviewed. You are mainly concerned about ensuring that they have a say in research so that it presents findings that they can use for equality issues and about ensuring that they can share their deeper and complex story with others. How would you design this study?

INDEX CARD EXERCISES

Index cards are a great way to garner feedback from students throughout the semester. Analysis of the content on the cards is an exercise in qualitative coding—how to quantify qualitative analysis—and includes explanation of the process and naming the terms for the feedback that students have submitted. This exercise also shows that the instructor cares about how students are feeling in their research process and it certainly cannot hurt ratings on teaching evaluations.

Following is a step-by-step description of the process:

1. Distribute one card to each student.
2. Ask a dualistic question, which contains both quantitative and qualitative components (do you love or hate research; why?).
3. Give students 5 to 10 minutes to complete the cards and then collect them.
4. Ask a scribe from the class to write themes and frequencies of particular answers on the board.
5. The instructor reads each card aloud. The scribe documents answers as counts, with hash marks for *love* and *hate*; then, using a different category for each response, the scribe records the text responses to the question *why*.
6. Count each love and hate hash mark to arrive at a total; see which wins.
7. For the qualitative answers, ask students what patterns they see. Interaction is important, and processing the qualitative responses can garner student investment in directing their needs in the course.
8. The instructor explains that the love/hate question is nominal and that frequencies were counted for quantitative data; the why question is qualitative and was coded for first-level (direct surface answers) and second-level (between-the-lines or interpreted meaning) patterns.

Following are suggested questions for card responses:

1. Do you love or hate research? Why?
2. Does research provoke anxiety in you? Why?
3. What do you want to learn about most in this class (probes such as data management, statistics, and results can be used)? Why?
4. Do you expect to have more knowledge of research before entering a research course than you would have in a practice class? Why?
5. What would it look like if research were easy and fun for you? Why?

FIELD OBSERVATION EXERCISE

Similar to the index card exercise, field observation exercises teach students field work, qualitative coding, and how to quantify qualitative data. In addition, it is fun to get out of class and apply research methods in a real-world setting. This is also a quick and easy exercise to reveal to students that yes, they can and do conduct research easily and effortlessly.

Following are the steps for this exercise:

1. Ask students to gather in groups of two or three. Although they may interact, encourage them not to talk or compare notes during the exercise to allow for more objective note taking and inter-rater reliability for coding across observations.
2. Ensure that students have paper and pen, laptop computer, or some sort of device for recording observations.

3. This exercise can be broad or narrow depending on the instructor's intent for student learning. If a broad approach is selected, simply ask students to document what they see for coding later. If the approach is narrow, ask students to observe certain behaviors, such as talking or interaction, to be coded later.
4. Send students out into the nearby environment (e.g., the Quad, Food Court, social work building, psychology building, or resident housing if the class is being held on campus).
5. Ask students to note the following:
   a. Physical aspects, temperature, noise, and persons at the location
   b. What is occurring (movement, action, participants, conversation)?
   c. Outlying observations that are perhaps uncommon to the area
   d. Anything of interest
6. Ask students to observe for an hour, and when they return to the classroom, instruct them to count frequency of major occurrences and observations, find the categories of observation (e.g., action, purpose, and behaviors), code the patterns within the primary categories, and present their field notes and interpretations of the observations.
7. Students can present their data and coding, as well as their quantitative counts of observations. Ask students to discuss the similarities and differences in their responses.
8. As students present their field observations, the instructor should comment on what they have said. For example, if all group members noted that people were in a hurry in the Food Court, the instructor would note that this is inter-rater reliability.

CODING TEACHING EVALUATIONS EXERCISE

If you are feeling comfortable with your class and want to increase this trust by showing your own vulnerability—and you're feeling brave as well—grab those piles of qualitative feedback from course evaluations and use them in a qualitative coding exercise. This is a great exercise for the instructor as well, not just to show vulnerability, but also to get a more objective perception of course and teaching evaluations. This analysis from students is very valuable because they can give voice to what the issues in the class were and are now; it provides them an opportunity to give the instructor immediate feedback as well as to practice coding analysis.

Qualitative feedback can be distributed along with your quantitative means and rankings (which is a perfect way to see if students have completed a Likert scale and know that a median should be reported, not a mean) for comparison with the textual feedback.

If the instructor is teaching multiple courses, students can compare text and codes across these courses. If the teacher has taught the same course for many semesters, evaluations can be compared in a more longitudinal study and plotted along a time line with codes and themes used as markers along the line.

A group of four or five students might analyze a semester of teaching evaluations, given time to compare quantitative statistics with the qualitative feedback, and present the findings to the class. Provide highlighters to code themes and request students to create a legend for the themes.

Remember to process the findings through discussion after student analyses are completed. This can provide the instructor an opportunity to determine if the same issues are recurring in the current class and gain ideas about how to alleviate such issues. A common request in the author's evaluations is that students want more real-life examples. This process gives the students a voice in their learning and helps the instructor to see improvements that students have made. The author has also found that a show of vulnerability endears her to students, and that students will even reassure her in the process. The instructor has become the client, and students learn how best to deliver outcomes to a client, social service agency, and even their instructor, in a research context.

Appendix

Sample Confidentiality Statement and Institutional Review Board Exemption

UNIVERSITY X SOCIAL WORK DEPARTMENT
CONFIDENTIALITY STATEMENT

Course & Semester/Year

Your Obligation to Maintain the Confidentiality of Client Records.

SOWK **XXX** graduate students will be creating databases, entering data, and analyzing data for local social services per requirements of their research project; it is of utmost importance that these records entered are kept in confidence and the confidentiality of their contents is protected. These databases will be de-identified by the instructor, _____, prior to the final statistical analysis as required for this course, to ensure the continued confidentiality of these records. For this reason, students must not copy, quote, or otherwise use or disclose to anyone any materials from any client records they are entering and analyzing. Unauthorized disclosure of any confidential information could subject students to sanctions.

YOUR CERTIFICATION
Maintaining the Confidentiality of Others:

I will not divulge or use any confidential information, described above, that I may become aware of during my service.

Student Name (Please Print) _____

Student Signature _____ DATE _____

Instructor's Signature _____

Student email: _____

Social Service Project Name: _____

*SEE BACK FOR RESEARCH STUDY DESCRIPTIONS AND EXEMPTIONS

SAMPLE INSTITUTIONAL REVIEW BOARD EXEMPTION

TEXAS STATE UNIVERSITY: INSTITUTIONAL REVIEW BOARD IRB EXEMPTION FOR THIS CLASSROOM RESEARCH PROJECT APPROVED SEPTEMBER 23RD, 2013:
EXP2013I379904I; EXP2013P996052Q; EXP2013W969490I

Graduate social work students undertake an archival/historical/ secondary data analysis and database development research study for local social service agencies as a gratis outcomes report and service learning opportunity, which is also a course requirement for SOWK 5323. These graduate students assist local social services in database management and information systems creation and then analyze this data to compile statistics and outcomes for the agencies to use for their own promotion and evaluation reporting. All data is secondary, already collected, and has been coordinated with this instructor to determine exactly what these agencies need in this sec-

ondary data analysis. Students have no contact with clients in these agencies and their course project is to provide useful information for the executive director's outcomes reporting as they see fit; this is the primary point of information dissemination. This instructor has met with said agencies for their requests for secondary data analysis purposes and this instructor monitors and supervises the students' database creation and analyses.

This classroom project falls under Federal Category 4: Research involving the collection or study of existing data, documents, records, pathological specimens, or diagnostic specimens, if these sources are publicly available or if the information is recorded by the investigator in such a manner that subjects cannot be identified, directly or through identifiers linked to the subjects. (Example: existing data, records review, pathological specimens.) (Note: This data must be in existence before the project begins.)

The data to be analyzed for this classroom project has already been collected and this data is information previously recorded by local social service agencies. Graduate social work students in this course will develop database management information systems, enter said secondary data, and analyze this previously recorded information. Analysis has been dictated by executive directors of these social service entities for their own usage and dissemination. All data will be de-identified by the instructor under the auspices and guidance of collaboration with the executive directors before any data analyses are undertaken by students.

In addition to the above explanation, this classroom project involves no risk to human participants since, essentially, there are no human participants involved; this project involves secondary data only.

Index

177